NETWORK MARKETING

— 2.0 —

REVEALED

HOW EVERYDAY MARKETERS ARE
RESHAPING THE INDUSTRY
FOR A NEW GENERATION

PAUL FINCK & DREW BERMAN

NETWORK MARKETING 2.0 REVEALED

Co-Published by
The Beyond Publishing
BeyondPublishing.net
and
The Maverick Millionaire Publishing
TheMaverickMillionairePublishing.com

Quantity sales special discounts are available on quantity purchases by corporations, associations, and others. For details, contact the publisher at the address above.

Orders by U.S. trade bookstores and wholesalers. Email info@BeyondPublishing.net
The Beyond Publishing

ISBN Hardcover: 978-1-63792-070-1

ISBN Softcover: 978-1-63792-086-2

Library of Congress Control Number: 2021914653

DEDICATION

BY PAUL FINCK

"No man is an island!" No one person can do it alone. You want to create something great, something bigger than you—it will take many, many people to make it happen. When I was younger, I didn't get this. I didn't understand what this meant. The more I experience and the more I create, the more absolute the phrase becomes. I, hereby, dedicate this book to the dozens of people who came together to make this happen. I dedicate this book to my family who believe in the vision and have supported my passions along the way to give me the space to make this happen; my partner in this venture who helped carried the ball to the finish line; our co-publisher who took charge of making this book known throughout the world; the many authors who came together to create inspiration and guidance for all; my mentors who taught me how to keep all the dreams alive and the projects moving forward against all odds; and our Maverick Universe community that includes some of the biggest hearts and best souls I have ever met. This book is dedicated to this inclusive NETWORK of amazing people who all contributed to make this one book a reality.

BY DREW BERMAN

For those who are on the journey to create a better life for themselves and for the others around them. This path is certainly not an easy one. If it was easy, everyone would do it. I honor and appreciate the mentors who have come before me and helped show me the way. In these pages, we can help share what we have learned and what we continue to learn from multiple perspectives. I dedicate this book to network marketers around the world who want to do more, be more, and have more.

INTRODUCTION

The world is changing! We all agree with this statement. As it does, we have a choice; stay the way we are and slowly fade away to insignificance or take the courageous move to change as well. There is nowhere this is more profound than in the industry of network marketing.

The industry of network marketing has changed forever. We are now in the next generation of network marketing we refer to as version 2.0. As such, to succeed, you must change as well. The old ways, old systems, and old processes will no longer deliver the same results. To be the leader for your company and team, you must learn new ways and sharpen your skills, or you will all too soon become obsolete.

At the same time, network marketing is experiencing a mega-growth stage. Over the next ten years, we will see more people enter the industry than any single ten-year span in history. Whether you are brand new, or a seasoned pro, the future is bright. Do you have the tools, the strategies, and the network to face the change and the growth with the effective balance of power and heart to position yourself as one of the leaders of the future?

In network marketing, there are countless benefits beyond the freedom and unlimited earning potential. With a low investment to entry, you are able to access amazing products and services, friendships, community, and personally grow as an individual. There also exists the ability to have impact and fun! We are excited to reveal to you all that is possible.

As you read through the stories in this book, know that these stories and people represent your current (or future) prospects, teammates, clients, best friends, and community members. You may see yourself in some of these stories, or someone you know. These people have been chosen to give you different perspectives on where the profession is, and where it is going. The contributing authors are here to reveal their stories to inspire, and to have impact. The ripple effect can be far and wide. We encourage you to share these stories with others. May this book offer you new ideas and new ways to stretch, expand your network, grow your business, and prepare you for Network Marketing 2.0.

Welcome to *Network Marketing 2.0 Revealed*.

CONTENTS

NETWORK MARKETING

2.0

REVEALED

CHAPTER 1

ANALYZE THE PAST, LIVE IN THE PRESENT, VISUALIZE THE FUTURE

Paul Finck

The Past

Company after company… yes, I have been a part of company after company over the years. The first network marketing company I was a part of was in 1987. I was young. I was good at sales. I was a serial entrepreneur. I was perfect as a prospect for network marketers everywhere. I was approached by the family of my girlfriend's friend, and I jumped at the chance. I thought I would make a killing. I signed up, went to meeting after meeting, and even got a chance to sign a few people as distributors. AND… you know the rest of the story. It happens in network marketing all the time. At some point, I stopped. I stopped without ever making any money to speak of. I stopped long before I even had a chance to succeed. Why? What happened? I was good. I could sell. This should have been easy… WRONG.

Now, nearly 35 years later, and over a dozen companies later, I know what happened, and I am here to tell you what that was. Do you want to know? Would you like to know what will help increase your odds for success in network marketing? I will tell you in the hope that this information gets to you in time. My prayer is that you found this message and, in turn, our community (The Maverick Universe™) before you had gone down to many dead ends and wasted too much time in the wrong place. I pray you receive this information in time to affect your future.

Now back to my past.

After 35 years as an entrepreneur, knocking on opportunity's door and getting rejected more times than I want to admit, the reason for NOT succeeding started to accumulate. The first company I joined was for my girlfriend. At the time, it seemed like a legitimate reason. I wanted to make her happy and make some money. Great reasons. I also wanted us to do something together. Along comes an opportunity where we get to sell skincare products and do facials for her friends. *Presto!* This seemed like the perfect storm. What could go wrong? Let me list the ways by analyzing what happened:

- My girlfriend didn't like sales and wanted to give away more product than she sold;
- My girlfriend and I broke up shortly after entering the agreement with the franchise, leaving me to build the business on my own that I got into for her; and,
- I had zero interest in the product or giving facials!

Back to the drawing board.

Almost immediately after leaving that company (finally), I was introduced to one of the big players in the marketplace. I jumped at the chance. I figured there were so many products, I could definitely find the ones I liked. Ones that I could feel passionate about. Another (what I now consider obvious) challenge appeared. I was sponsored by a person who hadn't created much success. I was too ego-driven to ask for help as a young man. The combination created the devastating one-two punch. I had no immediate support and was too embarrassed to ask anyone for support. Chalk up another failed attempt at network marketing.

Shortly after that, I was introduced to a technology network marketing company. Now, I had found gold! I loved technology, so this was something I could have fun with. I also had a great upline (they are magically still in the industry to this day as leaders) who really engaged me from the beginning. I started to create my first "TEAM". I plugged into all the local and national trainings and really found a stride. So, what happened here? I was still embarrassed to ask for help. I held onto my "know it all" hat a bit too tight. This meant I could only grow so far.

There was another reason why this latest opportunity was *not* the one… we were selling technology. For the most part, the perfect prospects purchased the product and used it… with zero residual or continuity sales happening. I realized, to continue to create success, myself and everyone on my team had to continually sell to stay on top with no real passive income opportunities. I clued in… consumable products and continuity payments are key to foundational success in network marketing. It was time to move on.

Fast forward to current.
What did I learn?

I did not know it at the time, however all these experiences and all the failed attempts at success were preparing me for success. It was teaching me in no uncertain terms what *did not* work. As such, I figured out what *does* work. Yes, there are key factors that you should look for to create success in network marketing. These factors do not guarantee success, nor do the lack of them eliminate the possibility. However, when you find this combination of factors together in one place, your odds are greatly improved.

To create a magnitude of success in your network marketing business, you should look for the following:

1 - Look for a product or service that is consumable or is connected with a monthly continuity or both. It is the ability to build up a continuous income stream that makes network marketing so attractive. It is only through the ability to create passive income over time that enables so many to make sustainable incomes over time. When you have a team of people feeding into this continuous passive income model, is how the abundance network marketing promises is delivered.

2 - Look for a product or service you have a personal interest in. One of the factors that makes network marketing work as an amazing distribution model is friends talking to friends (and everyone you meet), about this amazing product or service you have started using. The more you talk about it, and the more people you share it with, the more successful you will be! Imagine, talking about this thing every day for a month. You think, *No big deal.* Imagine talking about this thing for a year? You think, *Wow—okay I can do this.* Now imagine talking about this product or service every day for the next ten years, and you really don't care about the product at all…. *Wow, now I am bummed out.* When you LOVE a product, you will want to talk about it, and when you do, you create success. Pick what you love, and the future just got easier.

3 - Look for an amazing sponsor and an amazing upline. The core of network marketing is duplication. The more duplicatable the process, the more likely your team will expand. The more successful the duplicatable process is, the more likely the team will expand. The more you lean on *your* up-line to create success, the more likely your team will lean on you, thus helping to diminish the challenge of turn-over and burn out.

4 - Look for a quality compensation plan. What makes a quality compensation plan becomes the topic of long hours of discussion with little real conclusion. There are so many factors involved

to make it a clear process. There are some core factors to look for, though. You want a comp plan with multiple ways to create income, great new distributor retention incentives, and bonus payouts, as well as a great customer retention program.

With these four core components checked off, you will, at least, have a fighting chance to create the success you are looking for. Now, where do we go and what is the rest of the story?

The Future

We are in the best time in history to be in the network marketing profession. Corporations have run their course, and people are realizing little by little that the person who will look out for their future best is themselves … so why not work for yourself? We also have more and more people desiring to stay home and create their own destiny. More and more people are choosing entrepreneurship than ever before, and network marketing is one of the easiest forms of entrepreneurship to get into. Low investment, no education needed, no specialized knowledge needed.

To be successful—*highly* successful—in network marketing, it may take a bit more in the coming years. Although they *want* to be entrepreneurs, they have been burned, misled, and just outright lied to so many times, the majority of your target audience are tainted and thus do not believe you at first brush. Additionally, the average consumer is way more educated than ever. With instant access to the Internet, any product claim you make needs to be spot-on, or the consumer will find out in minutes or even seconds.

The solution is that you must be better at what you do. You must learn the techniques and processes that *work*. You will want to study and practice to get better and better. You will want to be the "go-to" guy they can trust to lean on. Then, they will notice you for the rest of the journey. Are you ready to "sharpen your axe"? Are you ready to be better than you have ever been? Do you want to stay in the game a bit longer... to cash in on the gold rush to entrepreneurship that is happening now?

Welcome to *Network Marketing 2.0 Revealed*!

Paul Finck, The Maverick Millionaire® is one of the foremost authorities in business and personal development today. In his over three decades of sales, marketing, and entrepreneurial experience, Paul has moved over $20 million in real estate transactions, sold over $30 million in informational products, and ran over 250 live events. With over three decades of network marketing experience, Finck now focuses his time on developing the techniques for the next decade of network marketers and bringing the process to the front lines for the masses.

He has coached entrepreneurs and small business owners from around the world to build their business and create abundant futures for them all. He has created success in a multitude of industries, including medical, dental, speaking, coaching, training, publishing, real estate investing, finance, informational marketing, distribution, and network marketing. Finck's passion for life is also evident in his lifestyle focus centered on his long-standing relationship with his wife and his six children - **THREE SETS OF TWINS**. When you desire a real difference in your personal or financial world, crave a strategic game plan, and are looking to build a great team and maximize your results dramatically over the next 12 months, Paul Finck is the Maverick for you.

Finck currently offers coaching to network marketers, entrepreneurs, and small-to-midsize companies on how to double their results. He appears on stages around the world speaking on using unconventional methods to build new businesses, create motivation, eliminate fear, and generate new business. He is available for public, private, and corporate speaking engagements, workshops, and seminars on a wide variety of topics, incorporating his **Maverick Difference** philosophy.

For more information, visit www.TheMaverickUniverse.com

CHAPTER 2

LIFE IS HARD. BUSINESS IS HARD.
NETWORK MARKETING IS HARD. LET'S START THERE.

Drew Berman

My journey started in 2001. I had just returned from an international bicycle tour in the year 2000. We cycled 35 countries from January 1, 2000 to January 1, 2001. I tasted freedom at 28 years old.

A few short years later, I was working in Real Estate in New York City, paying $2,700 a month rent for a 700 square-foot apartment in Manhattan. I tried to make it in Real Estate, but found that every deal was an ordeal, and I was running full speed on a treadmill going nowhere.

I was introduced to Network Marketing at a professional business networking event—BNI, actually. I met a man who dropped the big question on me. "Are you the type of guy who keeps options open for additional streams of income?"

He handed me a CD. I listened, and I was hooked. For the first five years, I actually did not make any money. In fact, I remember going to events with the diamonds to learn how to build this business properly, sitting front row taking notes, really wanting a solution to my broken financial situation.

My wife would call with the screaming baby, and she wouldn't even say hi; she would just hold the screaming baby to the phone. She was bitter, extremely negative, and it nearly cost us our marriage.

I was brokenhearted. And yet, I was optimistic. I was frustrated, yet I believed. I went from event to event excited and broke, event to event excited and broke. I read the books, listened to the tapes (yup, we had tapes back then), I went to the events, and I did what the up line said. Until five years later, when I had to call it quits. I wasn't making any money, my family was suffering, and I had to find another way. So, I did the unthinkable, and got a job. I would have rather pulled my eyeballs out with a fork.

Then, I found my second company. This time, I was ready. I was deep down the rabbit hole in personal development, and we went straight to the top. We started winning trips and breaking ranks, creating a team that was growing. It was fun and exciting, and I thought I would be with this company forever.

I remember my wife was earning about $5,000 per month selling Real Estate in New York City, as her mom was dying 90 minutes away in South Jersey. My wife would work around the clock, while being a new mom, and she was exhausted. Then she would drive 90 minutes to care for her mom. I remember calling the owner of our company on her cell phone and sharing my situation. I asked her what to do. In her kind, loving, motherly, nurturing way as one of my mentors, she said, "Drew, tell your wife we don't need her income anymore." My wife quit her job the next day.

Five years later, my wife thanked me. For what? She thanked me for when things were tough, for when her mom was sick, for when her mom passed. She reminded me that when her mom was dying, she had a year to care for her mom, because of network marketing. She had a year to mourn her mom, a year to get pregnant, a year to have a baby, and then a year to move to our first home in Connecticut. She didn't have to worry about mortgage or bills, because I dug deep, I worked hard, and I helped a lot of people. And because of Network Marketing, we had financial flexibility. Were we rich? No. But we had a really great lifestyle.

The magic happened. I had created a system at this point that allowed me to personally enroll 800 people and grow a team to 15,000.

I was implementing the law of attraction. I was working hard. I was focused.

I met a guy who was ready to make a change, and he happened to be a seven-figure earner from another company, and he was looking for a new home in Network Marketing. And I was the guy who found the guy. He was the guy we hear about from the stage. All you need is one, right?

It was a dream come true. It was the dream they talk about in Network Marketing. For more than three years, we made a full-time income from this one relationship. The bonuses were through the roof, my maintenance with him was minimal, and we were really, truly living toes in sand, phone in hand. We won trips to Hawaii, the Bahamas, Banff National Park, and one of my favorite trips of all time was at the Ritz Carlton in Dana Point, California. Those were incentive trips, and we were treated really, really well.

Then, my family and I took some world class trips to Israel, Greece, Switzerland, Italy, and Belize. No boss, nobody to report to, making good money and having fun.

Then, things changed. The seven-figure guy got into some legal issues, and his business volume disappeared... And I found myself starting from scratch. We were devastated.

Like life, Network Marketing has ups and downs. Tell me a business that doesn't. I've for sure seen the good, the bad and the ugly. Since 2006, I have made a full time living from network marketing, and the best years are ahead of us.

Fast forward to now. I have the honor and pleasure to share with people what I have learned, collaborate with amazing people who want more of life, and assist people on their journey.

A lot of my clients are confused about the future of Network Marketing. There's always a new social media strategy. A new app like Clubhouse comes to market. People are texting now more than calling, so human connection is needed more than ever.

I've seen people create extraordinary lives, and have seen a lot of people struggle. I've seen companies come and go. Seven-figure income earners join and then leave. I've also seen some things that most people don't talk about. The friendships that I've developed in the Network Marketing space are remarkable, and I wouldn't trade it for the world. Does everybody get rich in Network Marketing? Certainly not. It is a business like every other business. It requires focus, time management, grit, some magic, relationship building, sales, marketing, social media strategies, leadership, and a burning desire to succeed.

Network Marketing is going to go through mega growth over the next 10 to 20 years, and we are really excited for the rise of this amazing profession. The stories in this book will touch your heart and your spirit, and they will give you hope.

We've chosen these people to showcase for very specific reasons. Some are seasoned Networkers who have made over seven figures in a career, and some are just getting started. In these pages, you will see the heartbeat of Network Marketing. Some join for the money, but they stay for the relationships. Some join for the product, and they stay for the personal development. If you're considering Network Marketing for the first time, allow us to be your guides as you explore. If you're a seasoned Networker and want more, we can help you get from where you are to where you want to go.

If you have heart, a willingness to learn a new craft, and you are patient with yourself, you can create success as a professional Network Marketer. Network Marketing can be an expensive hobby or a lucrative business.

Here are some tips to turn it into a lucrative business, based on 20 years of experience:

Think bigger, believe sooner.

Treat it like a business.

Set goals that inspire you.

Work with a mentor.

Create a DMO - Daily Method of Operation.

Be a servant leader.

Don't get stuck on the learn, learn, learn hamster wheel.

Implement as you learn.

Find a great company.

Be loyal.

Spend focused time on IPA's - Income Producing Activities.

Recently, I won an incentive trip to Cabo. As I sat there with my toes in the sand, my phone in hand, I realized that was my brand. Network Marketing 2.0 is here.

We will assist you on your journey. I partnered with Paul Finck, the Maverick Millionaire, so that we can help more people have fun, have impact, and make more money. This is a lifestyle business. It takes hard work for sure, and when done right, it can be fun and flexible. Will you get rich? Not necessarily, but your life can for sure get enriched.

If not now, then when?

If not this, then what?

If not you, then who?

Let's make this profession even better, one Zoom call, one event, one book, one story, one person at a time.

Everything you need, you have, and everything you want is coming. Let's begin.

Drew Berman is an international speaker, bestselling author, peak performance strategist, avid traveler, triathlete, adventurer, and head of the Network Marketing Division of the Maverick Universe. Berman has personally enrolled over 800 and grown a team of over 15,000 with his proprietary simple system process.

He is focused on helping networkers with the skills, habits, and mindset they need to have more fun and flexibility in their business and their life.

When not running, building, and supporting his Network Marketing teams or speaking and training around the world assisting people from their first customer to their first million, he is home in Connecticut with his wife, Corey, and sons, Tyler and Noah.

After taking a yearlong, thirty-five country, 200-person, 20,000-mile bicycle tour around the world in the year 2000, Berman found himself BBB—"busy but broke"—selling Real Estate in New York City. Chasing the feeling of freedom he felt from his bike adventure, he got introduced to the world of Network Marketing. Now, after twenty years in the industry, Berman has seen too many people struggling. He partnered with Paul Finck, The Maverick Millionaire, to build the Network Marketing Division, which focuses on assisting people with the skills, habits, and mindset to create the lifestyle they want and deserve.

For a free strategy session guaranteed to assist you on your journey, visit www.callwithdrew.com

CHAPTER 3

IT TAKES HEART

Tommy Johnson

I had my share of doubts when, 19 years ago at the age of 30, I was approached with a business opportunity in the profession of network marketing. Although I had been approached many times before this time it was in a professional manner….sharing what it could mean to me and my family. There was no hype, no unrealistic expectations, or promises which had always turned me off in the past. I was not sure if a direct selling opportunity was for me. Together my wife Lindsay, and I, made a decision to go for it. We put our heads down and went to work. I've always set high expectations for myself and push to succeed at anything I've started. Part of my motivation was the number of naysayers that, like me initially, did not understand the business model. The excitement is in the facts and business decisions should be based on facts, not feelings.

That was then… today I can share that we built an organization of over 140,000 team members in 42 countries. We've enjoyed a lifestyle that would have never allowed the choices we've had because of the financial freedom that came with the decision, determination, and willingness to do what, unfortunately so many won't to see our goals and dreams realized. It's called treating it like a business.

Lindsay and I have enjoyed the luxury of being stay at home parents, never missing the basketball practices, camps and games with our son Jerry. Always at Sierra's drama classes, singing lessons, recitals, and plays. International vacations with family. Not to mention trips won to Dubai, Thailand, Rome, Venice, Iceland, Mexico, The Caribbean, South Africa, Hawaii, and more.

In less than 2 years I was able to stop working as a a realtor spending 12-14 hours a day working away from home. Instead, I became a real estate investor. Network marketing allowed us to never miss special family moments. Lindsay and I have always been stay-at-home parents and involved with their school activities and interests. It also enabled us to eliminate challenges many young couples face when raising children. We never had to stress about money, or say no to the sports and activities they wanted to participate in. It simply set us free.

I attribute my personal success to creating teamwork and synergism. We all bring different talents to the table. My passion is to coach and guide my business partners to identify and use their gifts for the betterment of themselves, the team, and the company we represent. Success in network marketing is taking your eyes off yourself and serving the needs and goals of others. As an employee, or a small business owner the focus is on your next step, your next increase in money, and moving people in the direction of attaining your personal goals. In my business, I quickly learned that when concentrating on helping others succeed, I did not need to be concerned with my success. I would have that, along with the many others that I coach and mentor to attain their goals. I have a passion for helping others condense their learning curve as it relates to building a successful network marketing business. It is simply too costly

to make all of the mistakes on your own. Unlike other business models, where it is you against the world, network marketing is a team sport.

Our success as a couple was realized by the way we learned to work together. One of the biggest inroads to success is complete support by your spouse. I do most of the front-end work. I'm in the trenches so to speak. Lindsay does most of the "behind the scenes" work...something that any business needs to be successful. She is an incredible wife and supporter. She's often told people that I am goal-minded...something I personally had not thought much about at the beginning. She's reminded me of the goals I wrote in the early days of our business with a time frame to get them done. We talk about having exceeded those goals and gone on, together, to change those goals over time and experience. I set a goal with each new person I bring in to my organization. Helping someone realize their goals and dreams while watching them develop as an individual and as a fried is incredibly rewarding. It's what I believe this business is all about.

As a first-time network marketer 19 years ago, I credit my success to having been mentored by a world class expert. He taught me how to evaluate the industry, what to look for, and how to follow a plan for success. By being a student, anxious to learn, it allowed our income to build to a lifestyle we never could have imagined possible. An income surpassing that of most small business owners, and CEO's of large corporations in America. But the greatest luxury of it all was the time freedom we would never have otherwise enjoyed with our family and friends.

When we look at superstars in every area of life it can tend to make us feel ordinary. I believe we make up for that void with "heart". I've always put my heart in everything I do and believe it has greatly attributed to my success. I first learned about heart when, as a young boy, I got involved in sports, and later, I repeated that in business through Real Estate sales. I found the same to be true in network marketing... you can move mountains when you put your heart in it.

It's been said there is more to business than the bottom line. I believe that when we make profit the last, but certainly not least, goal in or business and focus on making a difference in the people's lives we connect to we end up with a heart-centered business. It aligns with our values, allowing us to maintain integrity and generate revenue. I did not understand this as a young man, though I always had my heart in everything I did. Today, as Lindsay and I journey thru life as a family and in business, we have come to realize that "heart" has been at the center of our lives and, in turn, one of the most contributing factors to our success.

Lindsay and I were willing to put the time and effort in to this business, and sacrifice for a period of time while building, so we could have a life that gave us both time, geographic, and financial freedom. Success is a choice…we chose to succeed. You have the same choice.

If you have a dream and you are ready to step out and make it happen, reach out to me. I look forward to helping others enjoy the freedom they long for by sharing what we've learned with anyone ready to change their life.

Tommy Johnson. Born and raised in Phoenix, Arizona, Tommy Johnson is married to Lindsay. Together, they have two children, Jerry Ray, 20, and Sierra Dawn, 16. The Johnsons enjoy the benefits of owning a home-based business, which has enabled them to be involved with school activities and their children's outside interests their entire lives.

As a boy, Johnson was involved in sports and learned the importance of practice, consistency, and self-discipline. While he was never a fan of school, part of his ability to participate in his chosen sport of motocross meant his grades must remain at B average, or above. The lessons, discipline, and personal development have followed him into adulthood. Knowing from a young age he never wanted the confinement and limitations, of a traditional job, Johnson chose to go into real estate sales for KB Homes, the second largest home builder in the world. While he had the top sales of over 15 million dollars, he could only be awarded Rookie of the Year in Arizona, since it was his first year with KB. Winning every award available, his most coveted was the MAME Award (Major Achievements in Merchandising Excellence). Each builder in the state entered their salesperson, but only one out of all the builders would receive the award based on an intensive interview by a panel of eight.

Eventually, an opportunity was presented to Johnson in network marketing that made sense for him and his family. Utilizing what he had learned, his self-discipline, goal-setting, along with three years of hard work, Johnson and his wife were able to create a life for their family that has provided time, geographical, and financial freedom for the last 16 years as network marketing business owners.

Multi-Million Dollar Club member

Founder of the International MB30 Movement.

(Millionaire By Thirty)

International Public Speaker

International Trainer and Mentor

CHAPTER 4

DARE TO DREAM. CREATE A PLAN.
FIND A MENTOR. THEN DO IT.

Carolyn Johnson

"Why don't you just go out and get a job!" I laugh at it now, but, that was my response when my cousin, Bob, first invited me to join him in network marketing. It was 1970; I was just getting started in real estate. I had already had a hard run of reality, and I knew nothing came easy; monetary success came from having a really good job— better yet, owning a brick-and-mortar business. Whatever Bob was pitching, I wasn't going to have any part of it, and I curtly declined his offer.

It is funny. Life changes, and along with it, the way you see the world...

Nearly thirty years passed, and Bob reappeared. He was looking healthy, happy, and well-to-do. He'd been living an extravagant lifestyle, the fruit of his smart labor, and testament to his immense professional success. There I was in the same town he'd initially found me in— still grinding away hour after hour. To be sure, I had enjoyed a level of success, too, achieving things I'd set out to do. I climbed the corporate ladder and even owned my own small business. However, when Bob showed back up, I was drowning under a worrisome debt of $100,000 acquired after a failed event. I was upside down, had sold my home, and was renting a 10' X 12' bedroom from one of my girlfriends to recover some of the costs.

It was apparent that my diligent efforts and ambitious aspirations never allowed for true financial freedom— and indeed not time freedom. On the other hand, Bob was enjoying both. He had far more time and money than rightly seemed fair. He gently encouraged me to take another look at network marketing. I did just that.

By this time, I knew to trust Bob's leadership. He was serious about business, and I followed what he taught in earnest, putting his system in place and chipping away at my debt. When I think about the 10' x 12' room that it all started from; a bed, a dresser, and a computer table in the corner, it's astonishing.

With Bob's mentorship, I laid out a clear business plan, and day by day, little by little, I progressed. Within three years, my network marketing business efforts were amply rewarded with a seven-figure income— more than I made in the first 14 years of my corporate career, and I did it from home with no employees and no inventory! Hard to believe that you can start with no promises, no salary, no insurance, and no paid vacations —and end up creating a lifestyle rarely achieved as either an employee or small business owner. Seven figures. Three years. Stunning.

Does that happen to everyone? Of course not. But my "why" was great, and I was serious and dedicated. I had good reason...

When Bob showed up, I was fortuitously living in Phoenix, Arizona. My former high school boyfriend lived there. My first marriage hadn't gone well, so I left my conflicted life behind and decided to marry my high school sweetheart, instead. Change is never that simple. While my surroundings were different, I had brought myself with me, which included my view of the world.

My first marriage was turbulent in a way that I search for words to describe; none seem to convey it. Looking back, it now appears some cruel foregone conclusion that I would have found myself tangled in abuse. It was something I had grown accustomed to from an early age, and although terrifying, it was somehow perfectly normal.

As a young girl, I grew up in the scathing heat of my father's perpetual disappointment. He wasn't a gentle person to begin with; he was prone to drinking, and he had wanted a boy. I recall him standing in the doorway of my male cousins' bedroom when we visited. He'd point out that my room should have looked like that; baseball bats, soccer balls, running shoes.

It was confusing, and I was little; my presence seemed to make him angry. It drove me to please others; parents, priests, nuns, and most particularly, Jesus Christ, Himself. In my young mind, I thought if I could just make everyone happy, they wouldn't be so angry all the time.

God had given me a powerful will, but no amount of effort worked; kind words, gentle touch, laughter, hard work— none of it. Certainly, there were happy moments in my childhood, like anybody else's, but the fear of being attacked constantly hunted me. Meanwhile, the insults swam laps in my brain. "You're not pretty!", "you're not smart enough to do that!" You will never amount to anything!"

By the time I was a teenager, I was wholly tired of it all; I stopped trying to please anybody - even myself. God was on that list, too. As I looked at my prospects, college was never an option. I was to get married and have babies—plain and simple. By the age of 19, I made my father proud and married an alcoholic 12 years older than myself. That was my first marriage.

As I mentioned, it was rather fortuitous that I found myself in Phoenix. When I think of the symbolism of Phoenix, a universal symbol of rebirth and renewal; that fabled bird rising from the ashes; I realize God might have been up to something. It's the very place where I reunited with Bob, joined him in network marketing, and the dramatic turn in my life took place.

My life and struggles—a story of fall and recovery—is not uncommon to many women. I know now that no matter where we've come from or what has passed in your life, none of it matters. What matters is what you choose to do now. Whatever cards you were dealt before today, this is a new hand. We can choose to get bitter…or get better! I chose to get BETTER!

The gains in my life took hard effort, a willingness to leave the past behind, and a commitment to rejuvenate my soul with the goodness in the world.

Today, I view network marketing in a completely different light than I did in those early days. The truth is, network marketing has been a reliable, productive way to make money since the 1700s— long before they even had retail stores. When I hear the occasional distasteful comments about our industry, I think back to those days when I told Bob to "go get a job," and I laugh; people just don't know what they don't know. Network marketing has had its share of characters trying to turn a quick buck, but that exists in every industry; it's not exclusive to network marketing.

Network marketing is more than a career; it has filled my memory bank full of extraordinary experiences, expanded my knowledge of the world, enriched my life with precious friends, and has transformed both my self-worth and my net worth. These things are not derivatives of products, but, rather, sourced from the many kind, generous, and genuine people who held out their hand to help me up. They told me, "You are beautiful," "You are smart," and, "You are going to do great things!" That changed everything.

Wherever you live on this planet, you, too, can rise from the ashes, "like a *phoenix*"—and transform your whole world. I have seen it. I have done it. I am living it.

 **Carolyn Johnson**. As a little girl, all Carolyn Johnson wanted to know was how to be good. This little girl with an inquiring mind, and the young woman she became, rose from a background of repression, alcoholism, and abuse. Her early job experiences were marked by blatant sexist discrimination in matters of compensation and advancement. Through it all, Johnson was formed by adversity and her choice to remain positive and learn. She learned from big business, small business, and monkey business. She learned from failure and from success, as she went from the ashes of defeat to heading an organization of 175,000 team members.

Today, Johnson lives in Phoenix, Arizona, as a single parent of two incredible grown children, Cathy and Tommy, is a grandmother of six, and most recently, a great-grandmother of two! She enjoys the amazing blessing of working closely with Tommy and his wife, Lindsay, working and strategizing together on their individual businesses, and traveling the world in business. A dream come true!

www.CarolynMJohnson.com

CHAPTER 5

SANDI AND ED COHEN

We've yet to hear of anyone waking up one morning and saying to themselves, " I think I'll start a career in network marketing". Making that decision usually is a result of change. Something traumatic has happened in their life, which in some ways, was a bit of desperation. In our situation, it was just that.

In the book *The Road Less Traveled*, by Dr. M. Scott Peck, the very first three words in the first chapter of his book are, "Life is difficult."

Out of crisis comes change, and if your belief system is strong, things will often be better. We sold our traditional businesses in 1986 to a group of private investors who defaulted.

So began an eight year multimillion dollar lawsuit in Philadelphia.

It seems like yesterday listening to our attorney, saying to us, "Are you sure you want to move forward with this lawsuit? It could cost of your health. It could cost you your marriage. And even if you win, there's no guarantee that you will be paid! And then, he said, "No one ever said the law was fair!"

The eight-year nightmare finally came to an end. The judge decided that he was not going to do a jury trial, because the case was too complicated, and he forced a settlement. Sadly, it was almost eight years later, and the buyers were out of the business now seven-and-a-half years. The settlement that the judge forced was so small that the only winners were the attorneys. We were dead right, dead broke, and $450,000 in debt at the age of 52 years old. What would you do if you woke up one day and you were almost a half million in debt?

If you know anyone who has ever experienced a downward spiral, it typically gets worse before it gets better, and it sure did for us. In life, there will be obstacles, and you must be prepared for change. We were prepared to do whatever it takes to rebuild our life. We lost the 10,000-square-foot home, the Rolls Royce, the stretch limo, the English houseman, the cook from Grand Cayman, all were gone. We really never understood the pain of people going through struggle until we actually experienced it ourselves.

Rebuilding is not an easy journey, but one that must be taken if you want to get to where you want to be. Maintaining positive thoughts was difficult for us. We live by this quote, "You are where your thoughts are. Make sure your thoughts are where you want to be." Most days, it was difficult to have any positive thoughts. The more we learned about the subconscious mind, the more we understood that we had to find a positive feeling place. We practiced holding a feeling of joy for 17 seconds. It was the most difficult thing to do without allowing a negative thought to enter our mind, but we practiced, and we practiced, and then we took massive action in a new profession.

We were looking to live a life with joy and POM (Peace of Mind)—a life without worries. We totally understood that starting a new career would be a commitment to a huge learning curve. We were willing to do whatever needed to be done, in spite of doubt and fear. We became serious students. Back then, technology was VHS tapes, which transitioned into audio cassette tapes, which transitioned into CDs, and of course, today, the online world.

We would look at people on stages who were earning what we referred to as "gangster money", and in disbelief, we could not understand how they did it, considering they could not walk and chew gum at the same time. If they could do it, we had to figure out what were they doing, what were they saying, and be able to accomplish their goals.

There were no options but to do things every single day, even when we did not feel like doing the tasks that were required. You must be willing to commit to the process, knowing your destination will be achieved. It's important to improve your skills and learn how to solve other people's problems.

Successful people pay their dues. And if you're willing to do the same, you can accomplish the greatness you're looking for.

Developing new skills, no matter the outcome, helped us pick up the 200-pound telephone.

We did everything to avoid having a conversation with anyone about anything. We truly did not know how to start a conversation or build a new relationship. It's important in order to get comfortable; we did the uncomfortable until it became comfortable.

We understood that in order for us to grow professionally, we had to make mistakes and learn from them. As communication with people improved, we were able to overcome the fear of opening a dialogue. Since people are our assets, we improved our ability to build relationships.

We wrote our "success plan" for the next three to five years, with a commitment for a lot of hard work. We committed to CANI. No matter how painful, Constant And Never-ending Improvement was a part of our daily routine to create the results we wanted.

We believed true success was possible, in spite of the emotional roller coaster that we experience in the profession of network marketing. In any business, there are good days, and there are bad days. The only thing that counts is moving forward with improvement and believing everything is possible, if you continue to be committed to where you are going. One of my mentors is known for saying, "After seven years of failure, if I could change anything ,It would be to believe sooner."

The first three years in the profession of network marketing was like banging our head against the wall. We could not figure out how to choose the right company, the right product or service, understand compensation, and how to choose the right partnership with ownership that would not fail us.

We experienced 11 different companies in a three-year period of time, while learning lots through that experience. In the profession of network marketing, it's not about you. We are professionals who become problem solvers by asking the right questions. We identify someone's pain, and we determine if we have a solution to solve their problem.

Many people have come to realize they need a secondary income. It's shocking how many people do not understand the huge tax advantages of having a part-time home-based business. The law states part-time mean seven to ten hours a week, and it does not say that you have to be profitable to keep more of what you make just like the rich and famous.

One of our good friends is a tax attorney who specializes in home-based business tax law. He boldly states, "You have to be brain dead not to have a homebased business and keep more of what you make!" And so many realize that the "40/40 plan is not working. Working 40 hours a week for 40 years, and not live the "dream"!

It wasn't until 1995 that we "cracked the code" and hit our first homerun. The moderate success we had fortified our belief that network marketing was the solution to our problems. We were with that company for seven years. Then, the red flags started to appear. That indicator was the unexpected compensation plan changes that was negative to the entire distributor organization. It was the signal to move on.

In 2002, we moved on to a new company—a startup—that we said we would never do. Fifteen years later, after a magical ride, that company developed financial problems and proceeded to disappear. We never believed that could happen. Our team was over 700,000 distributors and customers in 51 countries around the world. We earned millions, because we helped others to reach their goals. We travelled the world and made lifelong friends. It was the royal treatment wherever we went. Gangster money happened through a lot of hard work and helping others to do the same, and the dream became a reality.

We are often asked, "What is the secret to success in network marketing?" Our answer, "The secret is: there is no secret." It takes the ability to handle the daily rollercoaster emotional ride. What we found out, after being exposed to a mental exercise, is that it is very difficult to maintain positive thoughts for any length of time. We would lie in bed at night, trying to maintain positive thoughts for more than 17 seconds at a time. It took a lot of practice. Success is probably 80 percent mental and the other 20 percent initiating business acumen.

The days of our traditional businesses with 36 employees, six trucks on the street, $500,000 in inventory, and one million in receivables are in the past. We made a choice to do something different that would leverage our time and create permanent retirement income.

We have entered a new chapter in our life and our commitment is to partner with people who are coachable, teachable, and hungry to be in a better place to live the life they want to live.

A big question is, "Are you ready for change to create the life you want?"

www.SandiAndEdCohen.com

Sandi and Ed Cohen have been successful serial entrepreneurs for decades, identifying business trends. They have a history of identifying trends with "first mover advantage".

With a commitment to helping others, they have created a team of 700,000 in 51 countries and helped 48 people earn over a million dollars through duplication and multiplication.

Both graduates of Temple University and in traditional business with five pharmacies and a medical and surgical supply business with a specialty in pediatrics, they built those businesses from zero to multimillion dollar revenues in a three-year period.

They are co-authors of five books on the Amazon best-seller list, as well as included in Maureen Mulvaney's best-selling book, *The Women's Millionaire Club*.

The Cohens are cofounders of ANMP.com (Association of Network Marketing Professionals) and on the Distributor Council of the Social Networking Association https://www.snamembers.com/optin-36773033.

Their primary passion is to shortcut the learning curve for those who are willing and coachable to start to live a five-star lifestyle. Most importantly, they helped countless numbers attain their goals and are now helping even more people worldwide to get more control of both their time and finances.

They have a love of technology and want to stand out from the crowd and help others do the same. Empowering others to accomplish more in less time is one of their many passions.

Every tomorrow is a vision of hope.

"You are where your thoughts are. Make sure your thoughts are where you want to be".

.

CHAPTER 6

3 KEYS TO ACCELERATING YOUR NETWORK MARKETING BUSINESS

Katharina Notarianni

There are three key tools we found that will really accelerate your progress with your new business. It's easy to overlook their value, and after I tell you all about them, they will seem so obvious and simple. It is exactly for that reason that these tools may be overlooked. So, let me explain what they are, and how and why we use them in our network marketing business.

The network marketing company you joined will provide many marketing tools, and it can be overwhelming when trying to figure out the perfect prospecting system. However, the clues may be right there in front of you. Close your eyes and take a moment to remember whether there was a specific marketing tool the person who introduced the company or product to you used which resulted in your saying yes! Something simple helped you see a future for yourself and your family. Was it a video? Was it sampling the product? Was it talking with someone else who was already involved in the business? Realize the process you were led through was simple, direct, and effective. That's the key. You, too, can be equally successful by literally modeling the person who recruited you.

Recognizing that we all like to add value, we all like to give more information, it took us a while to realize that it wasn't the information that sold the opportunity. The real magic actually happens inside the person. Ironically, as time went on, we realized that the fewer details we shared and the more we listened, the better our response rate became. In fact, we were trying so hard not to be a "pushy" salesperson, we made the mistake of going into too much technical detail, sometimes never inviting the person to buy the product or join our team. Eventually, we realized that our job isn't to get a yes, but, rather, it is keep it simple and share the opportunity in such a way that the person goes through an internal decision-making process where they conclude whether the opportunity is right for them or not.

The first key is to let the company tell the story for you.

The corporate video is essential – it communicates who the company is that produces the products, it tells the viewer why the product is important, and it explains any technical information in easy-to-understand terminology. Most likely, that video cost the company a lot of money to produce, is created by marketing experts, and is polished and works well with any device. Most likely, you also have your own company website from which to sell products and services. Is the corporate video part of that website, or has your upline made a fast start splash page that you can use that features a short corporate video? The key is to use the company video or splash page. A short and sweet video is perfect. It doesn't require a person a lot of time to get the idea of what the opportunity is. If they like it, invite them to watch a longer, more detailed video and ask them if they have any questions. If they have questions, you are ready to implement the next invaluable tool.

The second key is to use a three-way conversation to close your sale.

Nothing is more helpful in creating a sense of credibility than to have someone else on a phone call or Zoom meeting who has experience and sings praises for your product or service. Inviting your customer prospect to a three-way call with an expert business associate who has more experience than you do is not only advisable, it serves multiple purposes. When you first join, the tendency is to not want to talk to anyone about your new business until you know it perfectly. But you don't have to wait. Instead, recognize that you have an entire company of experts at your fingertips, whether it is the person who invited you to join their team, other associates you've met who you like, know, and trust already, or another person higher up in the organization who is considered an expert. They have more expertise, and, most importantly, they have confidence in five key areas: the company, the team, the product or service, the compensation plan, and, last but not least, in themselves. These five pillars of confidence are critical to develop, and for some, developing a strong foundation of confidence may take time. It doesn't have to take a lot of time, though. As you make it a priority to build confidence in these five areas, you will succeed more quickly. Lean on the person who signed you up, or build a new relationship with a fellow associate. If the person who signed you up is shy and reluctant to do three-way calls, or perhaps they don't have the time or lack confidence, then request an introduction to the person who signed them up and keep asking up the line until you find someone who is available for three-way calls.

Since we aren't all comfortable talking to strangers, if that is true of you, leverage corporate Zoom events and team meetings. Find out when the company opportunity Zoom meetings or phone calls are scheduled. Add them to your schedule, and when you are prospecting, after they have watched the short video, when they come back to you with more questions, invite them to attend one of your company Zoom meetings to get their questions answered. Your potential customers have the benefit of meeting others involved in your company, and at the same time, they get exposure to others interested in the business opportunity. They also get to hear questions and concerns voiced by people just like them answered during the meeting. This takes the pressure off of you to have answers. So, get in the habit of saying, "Let me invite you to a meeting where you can get your questions answered!"

When my husband, John, and I first started our network marketing business, we were overwhelmed with all the technical scientific information available. Even though we were told not to talk too much about the science, we didn't really believe that was helpful. We wanted to be knowledgeable and share information as we learned it. However, the fact is that we aren't the scientists who developed the products, and we got frustrated that there was so much to learn. That often kept us from sharing the opportunity. In retrospect, the best source of information is the company video, and the initial advice we got was most valuable – focus on one product, the best one, the most innovative one, the one that we—or someone we know—have a personal story around. Then, once we have our own story, make a testimonial video.

The third key is to tell your story - make a testimonial video.

I remember we were very nervous at the thought of making a video for public marketing purposes. However, we knew many people who were making videos on Facebook and realized perhaps it wasn't such a big deal. Within two months, we had confidence in our product and the science behind it and made our testimonial video. We had confidence in the leadership of the company. We had confidence in the company's compensation plan. We had confidence in the great team we joined. We even had more confidence in ourselves as we shared the product. Sharing your experience is invaluable. It helps your prospects overcome their fear they may be taken advantage of. It makes the opportunity more real. Having fun with the process of making your video is also important. If you are a people person, gather with friends to make the experience enjoyable and memorable. Isn't it interesting how memory has a way of filtering the details of the past? Make the video while you are filled with hope, enthusiasm, and joy from your initial experience, as we all are when we start something new. Your testimonial video becomes a record by which you can later measure your progress and review the details of your experience. The possibilities you see for yourself and your world communicate your inspiration even years later to the people to whom you are introducing to your product and business opportunity.

So, to recap the three keys that will help you accelerate your network marketing business: (1) make the most of using the company video or splash page to introduce your product or service; (2) get your prospect on a three-way call or Zoom meeting with an expert to let them answer your customer's questions while you are on mute; and (3) tell your story in the form of a testimonial video once you have your experience with your product or service. In the meantime, you can request testimonial videos from others in your organization. These all add to your credibility and will give you confidence when interacting with your new customers, as well as help you create the success you deserve!

 **Katharina Notarianni.** Bestselling author and publisher Katharina Notarianni, together with her husband, John Notarianni, is focused on building successful residual income businesses to share remarkable products that have helped them balance the body, mind, and spirit. Their success story is featured in *The Network Marketing 2.0 Revealed!*, co-authored with Drew Berman - Network Marketing Guru, Paul Finck - The Maverick Millionaire, and several other successful network marketers. Ever the entrepreneur, Katharina Notarianni launched Healing Time Books, a publishing company with a mission to help authors make the most of today's digital technologies to self publish their works. HTB Website Design provides mobile-friendly website design services. And, for over twenty-five years, Katharina Notarianni, as The Tara Channel, together with her husband, John, has helped guide others on their personal journey of self-realization to transform their health and wellness.

www.BodyMindSpirit.online

CHAPTER 7

THE 5 SECRETS TO SUCCESS IS IN NETWORKING MARKETING

Pat Alva-Kraker

Entrepreneurship is in my blood. It began as young girl growing up in El Paso, Texas. My sister, Corina, and our neighbor, Gussie, and I created a game of "business" that we conducted off of two TV tray tables. One had a register and receipts, the other an industrial supply catalog provided by our dad, who sold industrial supplies. Gussie was the boss with his "office" on his front porch.

The cash register was my favorite toy growing up, outside of the Susie Bake Oven. I'd take the orders over the phone, write it up, then walk next door to Gussie's office for approval. Our customer, played by Corina, would come to the "store" to pay and pick up her order.

I fell in love with the art of doing business. My passion was birthed. Looking back over your childhood, when was your passion first revealed to you?

I didn't immediately go into entrepreneurship after college, although the whisper in my ear to follow my passion was always there. I followed a different path before I reconnected with my passion. This happens to a lot of women. We are steered away from a childhood passion by society, family, the community, etc. My outside influence came from teachers. After graduating from the University of Texas at El

Paso with a BBA, I spent over 35 years working for IBM and Lockheed Martin Aeronautics.

I launched my part-time life coaching business while working in corporate. It transitioned into full-time business after retirement at the age of 58. Within three years, it expanded to include real estate private lending and network marketing. I say all this to share one of the many lessons you'll receive in reading my story. Live your passion.

A leader practices self-care daily.

Self-care is a set of activities you practice daily that supports the lifestyle you've always dreamed of; activities that keep you healthy, feed your soul, and expand your mind. In order to do your best work as a network marketer, it is important to stay healthy. When I started my network marketing business, I was burning the candles on both ends. I had no life. I was working my coaching business and network marketing business. I began to tire. I wasn't bringing my best self to either business. Worst of all, I was sleep deprived. You can only go so far before your body starts talking to you. Mine did, plus I wasn't having fun in my life. I began to create boundaries around my businesses. I went to bed earlier, ate better, and exercised. I began to schedule time with my friends for coffee and date nights. Nurturing those connections that bring me joy. What good is it to be successful if you don't have the time to enjoy the simple pleasures of life. Find time to exercise, be still, enjoy a nice leisurely dinner with family and friends. Self-care can be easy and simple, such as buying yourself flowers, a long bubble bath, sleeping in, or anything that brings a smile to your face. Make self-care a priority.

A leader begins her day with an empowering morning routine.

The first hour of your morning can be the most powerful one. I am an advocate of having an empowering morning routine. The truth is you have a morning routine. Is it an empowering one? Do you look at your phone first thing in the morning while in bed, do you press the reset key on your alarm, or make a dash to the coffee maker? Yup, that's your routine. I didn't always have an empowering routine. In my past, I was getting up at 4:30 a.m., showering, eating breakfast on the road, and driving for an hour and 15 minutes. Not very empowering, right? Today, I wake up according to my body clock and follow my empowering routine religiously. Here's what my morning routine looks like now.

1. Meditation
2. Saying affirmations out loud
3. Reading my goals and visualizing my day
4. Identifying the three things I need to do today to reach my goals
5. Exercising
6. Learn something new (listen to a podcast, read, or watch a YouTube video)
7. Journaling. I answer these questions: what went well? what did I learn? and what will I do differently?

The benefits of an empowering morning routine include:
- feeling centered and empowered
- waking up energized and focused
- being in a state of gratitude and forward movement

Create a morning routine that resonates with you. Keep it simple, try different activities, and be consistent. Use some of the elements from my routine to get started. You can create a routine that takes 15 to 30 minutes.

A leader consistently invests in herself.

I believe in "constant and never-ending improvement", a term coined by Tony Robbins. I consistently invest in myself. I learned that the success in my business is directly connected to my personal growth.

Attending network marketing conferences, reading books, listening to podcasts, and hiring a coach are a few ways to invest in yourself. This industry is known for providing the best personal development activities. Set the example in your team. Attend all the company events and trainings. However, don't over learn. It's easy to say, "Once I know XXY, and z, I'll start making the phone calls. Learn as you go! Learn, apply, and teach.

A leader doesn't allow the emotions to run the show.

When I first entered network marketing, I was so afraid to fail, afraid to get rejected, and afraid to make mistakes. The emotion of fear kept me from taking action. I'd make all kinds of excuses for not picking up the phone, and at the end of the day, it was all about fear. Once I discovered this about myself, I began to let my actions be driven by results, not emotions. I was able to move forward. I'm not perfect. Sometimes, when I find myself dragging my feet, I have to stop and ask myself, "Is the emotion of fear driving my actions or lack of them?" If the answer is yes, I pivot.

A leader lives her life through intention.

Early on in my corporate career, I learned the importance of living a life through intention. When you set an intention, you are asking the Universe for a specific outcome associated with an event, along with the feelings you want to experience. I set an intention for everything that I do, and my results are amazing. This is a practice that I learned from one of my coaches. I use this process every time I call a prospect or schedule a three-way with my upline.

Below are the questions you can ask yourself when setting an intention.

1. What is my intention? My intention is to (fill in the blank). Be specific in your outcome.
2. How do I want to feel? I want to feel (fill in the blank).
3. How do I want the other person to feel? I want them to feel (fill in the blank).

Complete it with "and so it is". Detach from the outcome, and allow the Universe to give you your desired outcome or something better.

Success Secrets

The success secrets I have shared with you have contributed to my success as a leader, entrepreneur, wife, sister, and friend. I ask that you take one of the secrets I have shared with you and practice it for 30 days. Be consistent and disciplined.

These practices are part of a set of self-leadership principles found in my book; *Katherine's Quest; A Woman's Journey to Elation.* You can order this book and learn more about my services at – MajesticCoachingGroup.com

The passion of "business" first discovered as a child has evolved into working with women entrepreneurs to develop their self-leadership skills. Most are women who have plateaued in their business and want to express their passion and elevate their business. After working with me, my clients experience an increase in profits, greater productivity, and increase in team performance.

 **Pat Alva-Kraker.** Pat Alva-Kraker is an award-winning serial entrepreneur with businesses in business coaching, real estate private lending, and network marketing. Alva-Kraker has combined 35 years of IT experience, 10 years in real estate and certifications in project management and coaching to create a business that assists heart-centered women entrepreneurs scale their IT or real estate business with ease and grace, so they can experience time and financial freedom and create a life they love. Alva-Kraker is an international speaker and trainer. She is the author of Amazon's #1 bestselling book *Katherine's Quest: One Woman's Journey to Elation*. She lives in Fort Worth with her husband, Mitch and their dog, Dakota. She loves to travel, cook, and read.

www.MajesticCoachingGroup.com

CHAPTER 8

GO ALL IN

Colleen Rekers

Okay! Here's the real deal!

Let's talk! You've heard the saying, "You miss 100 percent of the chances you don't take." Well, I was that girl for years who said no to opportunities.

I have always been all about supporting entrepreneurs, especially moms working a side hustle, doing what they need to do or want to do to provide for their family or even just have a little fun.

I was the one at all the parties, ordering one thing or another, even if I didn't need it. I was also that person who said "NO" hundreds of times to the invites to join someone's team and be part of the network marketing or direct sales culture. I had my line down, "I'm happy to support you, cheer you on, and buy from you, but please, I don't want anything to do with the business-it's just not for me." For years, repeatedly, I would not even look at the business opportunities presented. I knew when that part of the presentation started, it was the perfect opportunity for me to run to the bathroom or head for the snacks.

However, one day, something changed. I found myself using a product that I knew I loved and that I'd use for life—it was that flipping good. Through these products, I found health, lost 150 pounds, but more importantly, found myself . . . my energy, my passion for life. I found a community where I could be unapologetically me. I found myself with high vibe, positive, amazing friends from across the world. It may have started with a product, but it was so much more. I had changed. I realized that I had never felt better mentally or physically.

It was then that I began to watch others in the industry. I quickly realized it wasn't what I had thought it was, or at least it didn't have to be. It wasn't high pressure sales; it was about sharing my love for something that had been life-changing. People were asking me about my transformation, so why was I so resistant to share? I just didn't want to be that person—you know the one: the one people run from or avoid, because they don't want to be propositioned for a sale or looked at as a potential recruit. And even though my eyes were opened, and my preconceived ideas were being unproven about this profession, I still wasn't convinced that it was for me. I mean I'm busy, I'm a mom of seven, with a corporate job, other entrepreneur ventures, and interests.

I spent over six months behind the scenes studying the compensation plan, watching the leaders, some of whom had far exceeded and obtained financial rewards, in amounts it took me several years to make. I even spent time looking into other companies in detail to compare what they had to offer, and how their company was run. For me, it was important for me to be educated and well-versed about the company, the industry, and the products before I jumped in. So, what did I conclude?

I realized that I had been saying no to an opportunity that presented itself to me time and time again throughout my life. I found that originally, I really didn't know much about this industry other than what I later came to understand were misconceptions and judgments that I had quickly made with not much thought given and with limited knowledge. I began to realize I could be authentically me, and by getting over the negative thoughts and limitations I created for myself, I could grow, expand, help, serve others, and change their lives like this industry and products changed me! You know what they say: you can't unsee things, so knowing what I know now, how could I not share, when this just might be what someone else was praying for?

I realized that the decisions you make when presented with an opportunity are bigger than you think—it could be a million-dollar decision—it could change the trajectory of your life.

Did you know that network marketing produces more millionaires than any other job or career option? Your race, your gender, your education, your experience, your socio-economic status, your political views . . . . . none of it matters. What career can you think of where there is a level playing field and everyone has an equal opportunity for success?

You don't know what you don't know . . . and I only know this because I was one of the ones who didn't know anything about network marketing but wrongly assumed so much. I wasn't open to learn at the time, and it's taught me a valuable lesson about the power in having a growth—rather than fixed—mindset.

Everyone thinks the reward, the goal, in network marketing is money. However, I have found that the freedom and the personal growth you receive far outweighs the money. In the end, you are not only enhancing your life, but you are also helping transform the lives of others. If I can be more, then I can do more, and ultimately, give more.

I've gone from a girl who said no to opportunities to a woman who realizes she is limitless, and this is the best profession both personally and professionally that you can undertake.

This career isn't for everyone, and you need to be realistic about your level of commitment.

If you dabble, then it's like a hobby, and as we know, our hobbies don't make us much money, if any. There is only one guarantee in this industry: your success, your reward, the money you make, is a direct reflection of the time and energy you put in. But isn't that freeing? You can choose what you want your paycheck to be, you can choose the time and energy you put into doing the work, and you can choose the location of where you want to work from. This is a job where you are your own boss! It's not dictated by corporate America or some company where you are looked as a number, or as replaceable.

If you're willing to get out of your own way, control those negative, limiting beliefs, and put in the work, you can accelerate your success. What do I mean by that? I mean that a job that took you 40 years to grow your income, not to mention the years of college or the other things you did to get to where you are today, with this business, you can cut that time down exponentially. How fast you rise, your income level, there is no time limit, no ceiling—it's up to you.

It's okay not to aspire to be a top earner. It's okay if $100 a month makes a big difference for you, and that's what you need! This profession meets you where you are at, and is customizable to your lifestyle. Don't compare yourself to others; we are all in different parts of our journey. Your journey is different than everybody else's, but remember: if you seek to be one of those top earners, you have to put in the work of a top earner. And if you are not where you want to be within this profession, it's on you, too! Not the company, the product, the industry, or your upline.

Now, I've grown even more, and I'm successful in multiple entrepreneurial businesses, several of which are in the network marketing arena. I am proud that I've stayed the course, learned what I didn't know, and am now able to carve the path for others to gain their individual success as well.

The key tips I can share for success are: Believe in yourself! Believe you are brilliant! Work on your mindset, lean in to those who have gone before you, be coachable, and do the work. This is a job, and you have to treat it like a job. With your belief, your work ethic, your desire, your focus high, you will be unstoppable and your potential for success limitless!

Dive into the culture, the community. This industry is full of real people, the most motivational entrepreneurs and dreamers with work ethic like no other.

The three biggest myths—or, as I call them, excuses that I've heard—I'm not a salesperson, I'm an introvert, I don't know anyone who would be interested, and I don't have time. If this is you, or if you hear this from others, I invite you to connect with me, so that we can dispel these untruths and move you beyond these excuses and into action.

I hope that my journey, the lessons I learned along the way, and the fact I went from highly skeptical and full of excuses to an extremely successful entrepreneur, a strong, independent mompreneur who lives out my passion in helping others to design their best life inspires you to say YES, and GO ALL IN!

 **Colleen Rekers** is an innovative transformation leadership coach, dynamic speaker, international best-selling author, and serial entrepreneur, living the laptop lifestyle, and running multiple lucrative businesses. She is certified life and wellness coach, an Integrative Health Practitioner, and an expert in several healing modalities. Her training, education, research, and life experience has catapulted her in the life, wellness, mindset and personal development areas. With her unshakable belief and dedication to her clients, their success is evitable.

Rekers resides in northern California with her family of nine, and passionately serves clients all around the world. Rekers is known as a Supermom for her ability to empower women to obtain a higher degree of personal, professional, and financial freedom, allowing them to overcome overwhelm, find joy, and show up confident and stronger than ever for themselves and their families.

www.ColleenRekers.com

CHAPTER 9

"THE MORE THINGS CHANGE, THE MORE THEY STAY THE SAME"

Janet Metzger

Having been born and raised in Madison Wisconsin, let's just say I wasn't very cosmopolitan. The Network Marketing and Direct Selling industry changed that for me. I have traveled to all 50 states, have been to 4 of the 7 continents, [and will travel to all 7] met celebrities, and I have friends all over the world. To say that the industry has changed my life, is an understatement.

For 18 years I worked for the largest Direct Selling company in the world. I was responsible for 25 corporate employees and over 12,000 independent contractors. Annual revenue was north of 60M. It truly was a great gig, that unfortunately came to an end due to "re-sizing". The hardest part of losing my corporate position was I had lost my identity. I didn't know what I wanted to be when I grew up, because I honestly thought I would be there until I retired. It took me 10 years to figure it out what was next for me.

After trying a few corporate careers and losing 2 more jobs due to budget cuts, I said enough is enough. I knew I had to do what I loved, and that was Network Marketing. I wasn't sure what that would look like or what I would do, I just knew that is where I belonged. For me it was like this, "You can take the girl out of Network Marketing but you can't take Network Marketing out of the girl!"

I had a ton of knowledge and experience, and kept up with the industry during my absence. I stayed in touch with the great leaders that had mentored me, so I felt I was ready to jump back in and not skip a beat. I researched companies, interviewed uplines, attended several opportunity meetings, you name it I did it. Nothing felt like a match for me.

As you can imagine, after that many years in the industry, I had thousands of connections, made hundreds of good friends, and was considered a mentor [their words] to hundreds of people. They still came to me for guidance, advice and inspiration, even after 10 years. I loved this part of the business…helping others to achieve their goals and dreams. I quickly realized that this is what I needed to do. I needed to go back into the Coaching, Mentoring and Development side of the business.

Tipping point #1 Social media is the start, relationships are the art

The biggest change that had happened during my absence was the evolution of Social Media. All you have to do is turn on any platform and you will see ads, and posts that promote the business. They say you don't need to talk to anybody, just post and they will come. Even if you are shy, even if you don't want to talk to anybody in person or on the phone, you can build a 6 or 7 figure income. When your Mom said , "If it seems too good to be true, it is." Well, that is the case when someone or some ad says this! The fact remains, whether you meet someone in person or on Social Media, you must develop a relationship. Relationships happen thru conversations. People join a business, and buy from people, not companies.

Learning how to network and build relationships are key skills that Network Marketers must master if they want to build a strong and profitable business. Working alongside a mentor can cut your learning curve quickly. In no time you can become a Master at networking and building relationships.

Tipping point #2 Become boringly consistent working your business

Our society has become what I call a "Microwave World". We want and expect things to happen fast, without little effort. We want to pop out a post, message people and just like that they will say yes. It doesn't work that way. It's like diet and exercise. You need to be mindful and work consistently on your health. You can't go to the gym one day and expect it to last for the rest of the month. You can't expect to work your business here and there and expect it to be healthy.

Think of someone who is building a home. They first start with a blueprint of what the home will be like when it is finished. All the measurements and details are planned out. Once the plan is set, they will go to work. They will start with the foundation, which is the most important part. They take their time pouring the concrete and make sure that it is exactly right. They refer back constantly to the blueprints, checking in with each step that is involved in building. If the soil is not just right, they will adjust. The home you are building doesn't change, but you have to adjust. This is just like your business. When you know what it is that you really want to accomplish in your business, you are part way there.

Like a home that you are building, you need to put the hammer to the nail and get to work. This is another thing that hasn't changed. You have to develop the habit of working your business consistently. When I say consistently, I don't mean constantly. You need to decide how much time each week you can devote to building your business. Maybe it's 10 hours a week. Let me be clear…when I say working on your business, I mean actually having conversations with people about the business. They might be current team members, customers or potential customers or team members. I don't mean stalking on social media, answering emails, creating different things for the business, I mean building relationships!

What do I mean by consistently? Many Network Marketers pick one day a week, and go full on. They spend 10-12 hours one day of a weekend working on their business. The other 6 days…they do nothing. Imagine if you tried to improve your health this way. You're not going to be healthy, you're going to be sore, tired and hungry! Instead, schedule 4-5 days per week for 1-2 hours a day that you are going to spend building relationships, and ultimately your business. Putting it on a calendar, greatly increases your chances of you building a habit of consistently working your business. You will be more successful if you do this…Be boringly consistent and you will not only be more productive, you will have better results. A little bit 4-5 days a week will help you to build a healthy business. You still need to put the work in, this hasn't changed! A trusted coach or upline can support you with this.

Tipping point #3 Know the why

Back in the day, I was often asked "How do I get people to work their business? They have so much potential, if they only did this or that." I still get this question today…and the answer is still the same. YOU CAN'T!

New leaders fall into the trap of doing it for their team members. If they don't do it for them, nothing happens. They say "I will do it for them, it's just faster if I do it. I need to build leaders and this way I can add another leader." You need to help them, not do it for them. Doing it for them, is a short- term fix…You will never truly be successful using this method.

You have made the business about you, rather than about the team member. Ask yourself, do you know what they want out of the business? Why did they join, what are they working toward, what's their WHY?

When you truly have uncovered their WHY, you have made the business about them. When it is about them, there is a better chance that they are inspired to go to work on their business. Uncovering someone's WHY is a vital skill that you will need to master if you want to become a stellar Leader. When you make it about them, and have learned to keep their goals in front of them, you won't need to get anybody to do anything. They will be inspired to win. Remember, you can't want it more for them than they want it for themselves!

You are part of the best industry on the planet. What other industry gives you an opportunity where the sky is the limit? When you truly decide with all of your heart that you are going to be successful, there is only one thing that can stop you. For most of us that have struggled in the business, that one thing is us! When you develop the necessary skills, your belief in yourself will soar. When you believe in yourself, you can't be stopped! Here's to you achieving all your goals and dreams.

Thank you for the opportunity to serve.

Hey, There! I'm Janet. Certified Coach and Consultant Helping to reduce turnover by up to 50%. I am an experienced Network Marketing Coach and Consultant with a demonstrated history of achieving stellar results. Having been a leader in various organizations, my experience varies from start-up businesses to Fortune 100 Companies. I have led sales teams that produce $60M in annual revenue and large teams of over 10,000 members.

I am highly skilled in all aspects of Network Marketing…from A-Z. Whether it be Becoming an Inspirational Leader, Business Planning,

Coaching, Development of Leaders. or Sales and Recruiting, I can fulfill the need. My style is flexible…I don't use a cookie-cutter approach.

I am a Subject Matter Expert in Network Marketing and Direct Selling having worked at the corporate level for 17 years, and several years building my own business. With a diverse background, my other experiences include Retail Management, Non-Profit Management. Distribution and Industrial Sales, Events, and Advertising. My first love is Network Marketing and is proud to be a part of this great industry.

www.CoachJanetM.co

CHAPTER 10

MY FIRST YEAR IN NETWORK MARKETING

Vin Sciortino

I am excited. What we are creating is phenomenal. I'm blown away by the concept, the structure, the team support, and, of course, the potential. I am more comfortable now than I was when I started a year ago.

It was February of 2020, right before the lock down. I was trying to develop and expand my reach from the many years of print and promo background. I was looking to establish new contacts in a very difficult market, due to the fact that print is something that is challenged with today's technology. Social media and all things web dramatically impacted my business. I've been in the print and promo business for years, sales and marketing for decades. Network marketing has never been a part of my life, but when I was approached, I was open-minded.

My primary stream of income has me out and about in networking events all the time. Pre-COVID, I would attend many meet-n-greets around the tri-state area. I am actively engaged with The Greater New York Chamber and The Rockland Business Association. Over the last couple of years, I've been exposed to networking of all sorts, and it is always fun meeting new people in multiple industries.

In February 2020, I met Drew Berman. The event where we met was one of the worst we've ever attended. The best thing about it was meeting Drew. I'm very excited about what we are doing, the choices I made, and the friendship we have. I remember thinking, *This Drew Berman is a good guy, and he's introduced me to great people, and my network marketing career is well under way.* I had open mind about it, and thought, *Hey, this could be a work from home opportunity to expand on my additional revenue streams.* I've always been open to doing that. I do embroidery, and some screening part-time on the side. I've done that already, so I've been exposed to additional side hustles for the last eight years, so I was open to this opportunity and excited about learning more about network marketing and what that could mean to me and my family. Through the year, we've learned so much from our online courses. I've met amazing people, and I am actually now a fan of network marketing.

Just learning about how people are able to grow their businesses in not a traditional way. Sales is the only profession I've known for the last 30 years. I was excited about the different opportunities network marketing would offer. The different ways to use social media and the different ways to connect with people, like doing a three-way call, are fascinating—this is a way of business I wasn't really exposed to in the past. Using your upline to maximize the opportunities and becoming, basically, a decision collector and rapidly going through the process to get to the yeses, you're going to experience a ton of nos, and the people who have the most nos are generally the most successful, because they've presented the opportunity the most, and they've given themselves a chance to be successful because of the exposure to the opportunity.

The concept of passive income— the idea of being able to make money when you're sleeping—is so exciting. I have two daughters, two colleges to look forward to, maybe even two weddings. Yes, I have reached a level of success in my life and business, and I know there's a lot more available.

In our company, there is a perpetual residual income builder™, and there are several different ways that it we can help you achieve the goal of being free, financially free. I just love saying that. It gives me chills every time. I guess I'm a freedom fighter. This is what drives all of us in this industry, and it is a very exciting journey. The possibilities are endless. The income potential is limitless. We are very lucky to be associated with an organization that has a brilliant vision and extremely strong leadership. It makes me feel that it can actually be achieved. If, of course, you are willing to commit and trust the process.

What is freedom? Freedom means the ability to pick up and go. Anytime you want to work, and from anywhere. One of my mentors and coaches in our organization, his brand is phone in hand and toes in sand™, which is pretty exciting. I mean that person can go anywhere he wants, work from anywhere, and do anything he chooses. He's my sponsor. Remember I mentioned Drew earlier—he's my sponsor, my coach, and my friend. It's nice when you have that flexibility for your family. You can provide for them without restrictions. It is a powerful motivator and worth the struggle for achievement. I'm thrilled to be in business partnership with him, a co-author in this book, and excited about traveling the world and having our families grow up together.

Walking on to a Division 1 college baseball program was a life highlight. I've always been pretty proud of that accomplishment. I was surrounded by guys who were really good players, and I did everything I could to make sure that I was a part of that each and every year for four years. You know, it's kind of what helped me stay in and be successful in sales, because of that persistence that approach, the ongoing battle to continually find ways to make myself better. It is well known in sales that there's a tremendous amount of rejection. It seems that way in network marketing as well. In baseball, there's a tremendous amount of rejection. The game is built on failure. If a successful hitter, a Hall of Fame hitter, would only have to get three hits out of every ten at bats to get in the Hall of Fame, the rest of them ended unsuccessfully. The hitter becomes what we call a right turner: seven out of ten times you hit first base, you make a right turn, you go to the dugout. So the game constantly challenges you. And if you can mentally get through that grind, that helps you with the bigger picture with life and all the adversity you're going to face. This especially holds true the last year and was pretty evident of the kind of adversity you can run into with no fault of your own. I firmly believe that my background has helped navigate sales through the last year, along with handling the ongoing persistent battle of getting knocked down and getting back up. This vicious cycle can tear you down if you let it. Network marketing like baseball; a 30 percent success rate is a hall of famer. If three out of ten join, that's a super star stat. That's kind of just getting on first base. If three out of ten who join actually build, then you have the beginning of a great organization.

If I can offer advice for someone who is brand new to network marketing, and was going to join, what words of wisdom would I give them?

I would say: be flexible, be coachable, and keep an open mind. Be a sponge. Be comfortable being uncomfortable. Be humble, and try to absorb and listen to people who are really successful in this space, so you can get closer to be like them. I think that's really something to be to your advantage, because it really doesn't matter how successful you might have been in your own industry. This is a different way and a different approach. So, if you're not coachable, flexible, and open-minded to what successful people have done in this industry, I think you are going to find it to be a harder path. This is something that I tried to do from the beginning of this journey. I try to be active with different webinars. I'm even a part of jumping on something like Clubhouse. I'm learning about maximizing Facebook with ads and things along those lines. I've been trying different approaches. I've started an Instagram account, because that is tied into Clubhouse and a way to connect with more people. Just like sports, staying focused and determined will pay off.

Have a persistent and consistent approach is key. Make every effort to see the process through from start to finish. That's one way that I always succeeded in sports, life, and business. I've built great relationships with my clients. I listen to my coaches. I create strong relationships. I believe strong relationships are the key, especially in sales and in life. Network marketing is a natural extension of that. That's probably the best thing that I can offer someone. I'm excited about my new career in network marketing. This next generation is going to be exciting. I'm ready. If you keep an open mind, stay coachable, and follow the system, you can be successful in network marketing.

 **Vin Sciortino** is an entrepreneur from the suburbs of New York City who has spent a career in sales and marketing. The primary focus of print and promo has now transitioned to include network marketing. Sciortino has a passion for helping business owners, networkers, and influencers all over the country add more value to their customers and clients. This has created additional revenue streams that are fruitful and provide stability. These relationships have had a positive effect on Sciortino's goal of helping malnourished children receive proper nutrition and the effort to solve world hunger. Sciortino continues this mantra in his personal life, getting involved in community organizations that also have the same values and beliefs. Sciortino receives tremendous support from his beautiful wife, Alice, and his amazing daughters, Lexi and Julia. Sciortino is available to teach you more about helping you achieve freedom, make impact, and thrive.

www.vsciort.ibuumerang.com.

CHAPTER 11

FEEL THE FEAR AND DO IT ANYWAYS

Pam Lewko

How does one transition from a being called a "wall flower" to being called the "Velvet Hammer"? ......Purposefully!

Being a leader came out of necessity for me at an early age. My parents divorced when I was young, and mom had to go back to work. That left the before and after school responsibility of my younger sister to me a great majority of the time. At five years old, my morning job was to clear the table of our cereal bowls, put them in the sink, lock the door behind us, and get us to school on time. At the end of the day, I then needed to make sure we got home from school safely. Once home, I would call my aunt, who lived about ten minutes away. She would come pick us up and take us to her house until mom was off work. Can you imagine this in today's world?!? For us, it worked.

My dad, God rest his soul, was an L.A. police officer. He knew hardly anything of being a dad, much less being a single dad. Many weekends that we were at his home, he had to work, but didn't have a babysitter. No problem, he just took my sister and me to the police station with him! We would race around that place like a playground. Crazy as this sounds, we would lock each other up in the jail cells and take mugshots of each other and fingerprint each other. Back then, it was kept on white card stock paper, I still have a two-inch stack of mine. At seven years old, we would go on ride-alongs, break up parties, watch people be dragged out of parks in east Los Angeles, and watch the prostitutes and alcoholics on wino street slumber around. As scary as it sounds, it actually wasn't scary at all. My dad would make a lesson out of it and would remind us that these people started out as kids, just like us. But through a series of bad decisions, or just one really big wrong decision, life took a left when they should have made a right, and this was the result. He would add that we were always just one choice away from being in a similar spot....so be careful of our choices, they were important. These lessons have served me in a positive way throughout my life. They have certainly made me quite independent and resourceful.

My mom, God rest her soul, and my husband will likely tell you that I'm bossy. My kids will say I have an opinion about things....most things. The folks on my team will say that I'm compassionate, kind, and speak the truth in love. I say I'm a leader who leads by "walking the walk and not talking the talk". I'm impatient, but extremely patient—confusing, I know. I'll never make money on the backs of other people, and I won't ask someone else to do something I'm not willing to do myself. My integrity means everything to me. It's something that took me a lifetime to build, and in a foolish moment, it can quickly go away.

Through these years, I would need to make decisions—and fast decisions—because of the great responsibility I was consistently carrying. It has served me most of my life, but there have been times where it has bitten me in the butt. I just need a little bit of information, and I'm off, without reading the directions or over-analyzing. That didn't really serve me when we were out to dinner as kids and they brought chocolate mousse before dinner....unbelievable! Well, I took the biggest spoon I could find and scooped a big ol' scoop and shoved it in my mouth... YUCK! I could not get it out fast enough, why? It was liver pâté that they *brought before* the meal. Have you ever dove into things that you thought were just going to be amazing and then shortly after, you discovered that it really wasn't that great of a decision? I realize now my first marriage to my high school sweetheart was kind of like that as well. All love and butterflies and I could escape my home life.....so I got married two days after I graduated from high school and moved 3,000 miles away from home. I wouldn't listen to anyone's advice; I thought I knew what I was doing. Only to find out that he got into drugs and affairs, and all I could think of were my dad's words. So, I course-corrected; I pivoted. These skills of my childhood served me well.

In the early 90s, I fell in love with network marketing. I joined a company because of a positive product experience, and one of the owners ran away with all the money. So the company collapsed. No problem, I pivoted, course-corrected with my can-do attitude. Some of the top earners from that company launched a new nutritional company, and I joined with my same gusto and rose right to the top. I was one of the speakers at their very first convention, and was part of the advisory team. I even spoke to thousands of distributors at the famous Pasadena Palladium. I had remarried and now had three incredible children. I was delighted that I could build a successful business with an incredible income *and* raise my children while working my business from home, and during that time, working from home was not the norm.

But there was a secret I was keeping. I was in a very abusive marriage, which, after decades, took its toll on me. I just got tired of fighting. Through the decades of ups and downs and keeping this secret, I got beat down and discouraged. My business felt the drag of it all, and it began to dwindle; it and I eventually just slipped away.

Somewhere along the way, this very capable little girl, who had transformed into a very independent, strong young woman.... over a couple of decades regressed into a wallflower. Have you ever looked into the mirror and wondered who was that person in the reflection and how did she get here? That was me.

I began to play small. I began to play safe. I began to be fearful of every decision, every situation, and every change. I just wanted life to be status quo, so I could not feel so on edge and rest, I wanted it to be "easy". But like Jim Rohn says, "Don't wish that life was easier, wish that you were better." Life is always changing, always moving forward, even if we are not. Time does not stand still for anyone. A seed grows into a tree, a baby grows into an adult, and I was growing in reverse and beginning to panic, because I didn't know how to stop it or turn it around. I got divorce and lost the belief in myself. I didn't believe that I was capable of running my own business any longer. So I took on a few part-time jobs, and we just barely scraped by for years. What happened? Where did that capable, outgoing, fun-loving woman go? I got isolated; I stopped staying curious and relevant. I stopped learning. I no longer took risks. My family was suffering because of my choices. If we aren't moving forward, we are actually falling behind. So, when the time came to pivot, I did not, could not, I perished…..almost.

Then, a friend cared enough about me to introduce me to a leadership and personal development company. She invited me to a luncheon, which started my journey back to not just myself, but a better, wiser, smarter, stronger self. I began to realize that I was worth it, that my family was worth it, that I *did* deserve it, that my kids were watching and learning to live in fear and learning to just give up when life got too hard. I'm forever grateful to John Edwards, who has become a good friend. At an event, he said, "Pam, why are you such a wallflower?" Had he not been brave enough to speak the truth in love and ask me that hard question, I may not have ever made the shift. I thought to myself, *Wallflower?! What the heck, I'm the girl who left the Kindergarten classroom on the first day and walked home across two busy streets because I didn't like what was happening. I'm the girl who bravely and courageously cared for my sister and I at such a young age. I am the girl who was the varsity cheerleader out there in front. I'm the woman who rose to the top of a company and used to speak and train thousands. I'm the mom who bravely and courageously raised three amazing kids on my own.* A wallflower? I began to see that I had become just that, but it didn't mean that I had to stay there. I made a decision that day that I was going to change.

Why now? Because I was sick and tired of being sick and tired. The pain of staying the same became too great, and it was time for change. When I began to boil it down, playing into my fear and playing small was really making it all about me, which honestly is just plain selfish. Me staying safe to avoid whatever I thought was going to happen was not only selfish, but irrational. If I think back to all the zillions of thoughts I have not acted on out of fear, because of what I thought was going to happen, I can think of only one time in these 60 years that the thing I was fearful of actually occurred. Guess what? We dealt with it. I didn't crumble, I didn't melt, no one took my birthday away, I am still here to write these words of encouragement to you. I just took the next right step and kept on walking. That's what you will do, too.

Now began the how! I developed a phrase, "Feel the fear and do it anyways!" Fear had a physical grip on me that was paralyzing. I trembled to even say my name when leading two people in silent prayer— seriously! I feared change, I feared confrontation, I feared failure, I feared success, I feared responsibility, I feared the unknown, I feared changing my circumstances, even though they sucked. I took responsibility and knew that "for things to change... I must change," as Jim Rohn would say. I realized as I started to change, things started to change for me. The definition of fear as a noun is, "An unpleasant emotion caused by the belief that someone or something is dangerous or likely to cause pain or a threat." It keeps us safe. But when it is an irrational fear or an untrue story made up in our minds.....it keeps us from living the abundant life that we are promised.

Because fear was paralyzing me in a very physical, mental, and emotional way and was keeping my family and me from moving forward positively, I knew I needed to have some physical strategies to conquer it. Here are my ten steps to freedom:

#1- I took a self-inventory and began to realize quickly when I was operating in fear.

#2- Pray! Immediately and constantly, "take all thoughts captive". Duet 31:8 "Do not be afraid, do not be discouraged."

#3- I made a little red stop sign that I laminated and carried around in my pocket. Each time I would "feel the fear", I would pull the stop sign out and physically say out loud "STOP!"

#4- Then, I would immediately move forward with whatever I thought I was afraid of. Develop a "do it now" strategy, not a "think about it" or "plan about it" strategy.

#5- Stop feeding the monster. Time and isolation feeds the fear monster and makes him appear bigger.

#6- I joined a community of women at my church and got really honest and asked for help and support. You're not alone. Find a buddy.

#7- Don't play the "what if" game and overanalyze things; it's just another form of procrastination.

#8- MOVE! Fear paralyzes actions. So....take a risk, make a decision, course correct as you move forward, if it's needed. Like my friend Noble Drakoln says, "Run and tie your shoes at the same time."

#9- When I "felt" fearful, I would jump up and down and yell, "I'm excited, I'm excited, I'm excited"!!! I realized that fear and excitement have the same physical feelings...butterflies in my tummy, tightness in my chest, a little lightheadedness, and trembling hands. So, I tricked myself and it changed me physically.

#10- Embrace change. Be okay with things being out of control. In reality, what do we really have control of anyways?

Fear is simply **F**inding **E**xcuses **A**nd **R**easons. Instead, **F**ace **E**verything **A**nd **R**espond! Give yourself lots and lots of grace, because it's not going to happen overnight. It will happen if you stay intentional about it and keep being brave and courageous. You'd be surprised who's watching you. When you break the chains of fear off, it breaks off of your kids, too. You will see them breaking free and others around you as well. Your family deserves it! You deserve it!

Because life waits for no one, an opportunity came along about a year after implementing the above strategies, and I was ready for it. When it presented itself, I jumped and was ALL IN! With this European company, we opened America! In a three-month period of time, I was one of only three Americans who qualified for the trip to Macau, China. It was a ten-day all-expenses-paid trip of a lifetime. On the last day, we had a few hours of free time, and I asked my colleague what he was going to do, and he said, "Let's go bungee jumping." The Macau Tower is the tallest bungee jump in the world. Little did my colleague know that I had a lifelong fear of falling. So, I told him I needed to pack. I was practicing avoidance. He said, "Come on, Pam, do you really want to continue to live life afraid? Do you really want to live life with regret? We may never get this chance again in our lives." I said, "I'll meet you in the lobby in ten minutes." Thank you, Rik Wahlrab, for speaking the truth in love and helping me to stay uncomfortable and continue to grow. It was terrifying, liberating, and one of the most fun and memorable experiences of my lifetime. Only second to giving birth to my precious babies. I am so glad that I "felt the fear and did it anyways".

It was at this company that I cheerfully gained the nickname of the "Velvet Hammer". I was the one who was willing to hit topics straight on, tell the truth as fast as I could (as my friend, Sarah Cranston, taught me), speak the truth in love, do hard things, talk about hard things, press in and press through. I became a "yes" person. Pam, can you do the presentation tonight? Yes! Pam, can you host the webinar this week? Yes! Pam, can you do the comp plan tonight? Yes! I discovered the joy in not hiding, the freedom in moving through the fear. The exhilarating feeling of being in integrity with myself that was so worth it!

Franklin D Roosevelt says, "The only thing we have to fear is fear, itself." It's a false story that's not serving you, so create a new story, one that will serve you. I now pass the baton along to you. It's time! Break free. Take a risk. Laugh more. Say, "Yes!" Live the life you are gifted with. Do the hard things. Make the changes. Drive the fast car. Be uncomfortable. Jump off tall buildings with a single bound. Your family deserves it. You deserve it. "Life doesn't happen to us..... life happens because of us," Grant Cardone. "Feel the fear and do it anyways," Pam Lewko.

Pam Lewko. Pam is one hip Nana, wife, mother, friend, lifetime learner, cooking enthusiast, beach lover, compassionate samurai, multiple business owner, retired wall flower, and a professional network marketer. She got bit by the Network Marketing bug in 1989. She says "bit" because she feels it's kinda like Spider Man, once it's "in you", you can never walk away. She stepped away for a short time, but she desperately missed the relationships, the team building, and the dynamic way you can be part of others stepping into their greatness.

Pam is a respected professional, with 30 plus years of sales and marketing in her background. She has built and trained sales teams all over the world. Besides being respected, she is well liked. Her innate ability to connect with people quickly, paired with her servant leadership style, has helped her to create dynamic results.

Pam is not only passionate, but is purposeful in her work ethic. She has powerfully navigated multiple challenging situations in work and life, earning her the nickname of the "Velvet Hammer". As the "Velvet Hammer" she gets things done directly, but with grace. She energetically tackles big goals and doesn't hesitate to reach out to her vast global network for support.

Whether Pam is running a team, running her home, or running a business, her innate ability to identify and confront obstacles quickly and decisively have created success personally and professionally for her.

Pam is grateful to have learned her greatest lessons in life from her children. Her children and grandchildren are her greatest treasures here on earth.

Her mission is to impact lives globally by helping others to realize that they can choose faith over fear every time. Pam understands this happens much easier when we lean into God for the strength and guidance to create incredible outcomes for ourselves, our families and our communities. Her passion is to transfer this understanding to each person who is ready to take the leap of faith and live their best life, with God as their Source.

www.pamlewko.com

CHAPTER 12

IS THIS A HOBBY OR A BUSINESS?
WHY DOES IT MATTER?

Benita Mairs

First, let me congratulate you for your decision! Someone showed you some information, at a presentation, in a video, or maybe a one-on-one conversation, and you saw value in the product or service and said "Yes" to an opportunity. Now it's time to be honest with yourself about the amount of time and effort you intend to put toward your new venture. There is no right or wrong answer to the question, "Is it a hobby or a business?" It's just a question you need to answer to know how this is going to impact your life and your taxes. If you have a full-time job or other full-time business and your intention is to order some products or use a service and occasionally refer those items to other people and make a little money, then your answer should be, "This is a hobby."

Your answer is important for two reasons: 1) when reported as hobby income, the income you receive from referring the product/service, reported on Form 1099, will be reportable on your tax return as other income on page 1 of Form 1040. It is not subject to self-employment tax when reported as hobby income. Any expenses you incur in the creation of that income are deductible *if* you file Schedule A – Itemized Deductions, and only up to the amount of income earned. You will still want to keep track of those expenses, however, the record-keeping may not be as daunting.

On the other hand, if you have a passion and desire to grow this into the amazing opportunity that you saw in your company presentation, there are certain things you should do to set yourself up for success and potentially audit-proof your business.

Let's look at what the Internal Revenue Service says about what qualifies as a "business".

Trade or Business

A trade or business is generally an activity carried on for a livelihood or in good faith to make a **profit**. The facts and circumstances of each case determine whether or not an activity is a trade or business. The <u>regularity</u> of activities and transactions and the production of income are important elements. You do not need to actually make a profit to be in a trade or business as long as you have a profit motive. You do need, however, to make ongoing efforts to further the interests of your business.

Part-time Business

You do not have to carry on regular full-time business activities to be self-employed. Having a part-time business in addition to your regular job or business also may be self-employment.

Example: You are employed full-time as an engineer at the local plant. You fix televisions and radios during the weekends. You have your own shop, equipment, and tools. You get your customers from advertising and word-of-mouth. You are self-employed as the owner of a part-time repair shop.

<u>https://www.irs.gov/businesses/small-businesses-self-employed/business-activities#</u>

Most people get started in network marketing while still working a full-time job (usually receiving a W-2 from their employer). Since most any business fails to earn a net profit in the first few years of business, the IRS is particularly scrutinous of losses reported on Schedule C (the form in your tax return for reporting self-employment income) when there are also W-2 wages reported. Therefore, taking the steps I recommend in my book, will help avoid the mistake the IRS might make by disallowing your Schedule C losses, and deeming them "hobby losses".

The most important things to remember are to always keep your receipts (or images of receipts) and making notes to establish the business reason for the expense. Basically, you are recording the who, what, when, where, and why of each expense.

Keeping a journal or a folder with all the receipts is one way to keep track of these expenses. Simply writing on the receipt, itself, is sufficient evidence to substantiate an expense reported on your tax return.

There are multiple applications available today to assist businesses with keeping track of such receipts. Most of these apps are available as downloads on your cellular device, such as, Expensify, TaxBot, and Shoeboxed, just to name a few. There are numerous ones available with different features, depending on your personal preferences. There are apps to track your business mileage as well.

Most importantly, be sure you are joining as an associate for the right reasons. Yes, there are tax benefits to having your own business, but it is only considered a business if there is a "for-profit" motive. You got in this business to make money, not write-offs, and to make a difference. If you make the commitment to really have a business, set yourself up right, be consistent, and follow your company's systems, you can create an incredible lifestyle and generational wealth.

Benita Mairs. Benita Mairs, E.A. (Enrolled Agent) is a tax professional with over 40 years' experience in the industry and the co-author of the upcoming book, *Accounting Made Easy for the Network Marketer: 10 Simple Steps to Doing It Right.* Following in her father's footsteps, she took over his CPA practice nearly 20 years ago. She has helped hundreds of entrepreneurs organize their bookkeeping systems and save thousands of dollars in taxes. But it wasn't always like this. She used to get frustrated when clients (especially in the network marketing industry) paid more to the government in taxes than necessary, simply because they didn't keep the necessary documentation, or know what documentation to keep, in order to claim these expenses on their tax returns. So now, she has decided to dedicate her life to helping you get your tax records organized the right way.

www.networkertaxes.com

CHAPTER 13

TRANSFORMING LIVES; RESTORING HEALTH, HOPE, AND HAPPINESS

Lisa Cassenti

To be a network marketing leader, you MUST believe in network marketing (NWM). I see NWM as a gift. It is the ultimate way to elevate others and "teach a man how to fish". Zig Ziglar said, "You will get all you want in life, if you help enough other people get what they want"[1]. This is the only way to become successful in NWM!

Here is my story to empower your conviction in NWM and begin a social movement to transform the "old world" view of NWM. Please remember my story whenever you hear that voice inside your head that says that NWM doesn't work. Tell that self-limiting voice, "Thank you for sharing. Now shut the FUCK up while I go change people's lives."

At the end of 2018, I was a single parent of a nine-month-old while working countless hours for a start-up company. I slept in between my daughter's night-time "naps", breastfeeding, submitting evaluations before midnight, and bringing my daughter to her father's. I was fortunate those days if I got to shower daily.

My parents kept telling me I couldn't go on like this. They were right. A perfect storm created in my body from the stress, emotional turmoil, and pushing my mind and body to the limits. On November

---

1 Ziglar, Zig. *See You At The Top*. 25th Ed. Pelican Publishing, 2000

5, 2018, I was diagnosed with breast cancer. The world crashed down around me, and nothing in the world mattered but restoring my health. As Tony Robbins said, "The person with good health has a million dreams. The person with poor health has only one"[2].

A few months into treatments and my life was falling apart. I felt like a failure as a mother, as I wasn't doing the "new mom" stuff I had envisioned doing. Dealing with cancer became a full-time job. I needed naps more than my one-year-old. The anxiety and depression that I had experienced for my whole life came back with intensity. Each morning, I braced myself for the deep discomfort that traveled along my spine when I initially sat up. Sometimes, I sat for a minute or two before getting up for my daughter while she and I cried together.

One day, a dear friend, Marina Cyran, encouraged me to go with her to a nearby yoga class. It was there that I met Kundalini teacher Darlene Attard. She knew what I was going through, as I had "the look". She approached me after class. She said, "Lisa, I know that you just met me. There is something important that I want to share with you. I can't promise what it can do for your health, but it can't hurt you. Are you open?" I was 75 percent open.

Darlene and her husband, Steve Attard, guided me through information about the NWM company they had partnered with, as well as two replenishment products. These two products appeared to me to be something out of a sci-fi movie or the future like computer chips that can store our life's memories. Darlene and Steve continued to share with me by introducing me to a compassionate doctor on the company's medical professionals board, as well as many people who were happy to share their own experiences.

One story, in particular, resonated with me. A young woman had been hit by a drunk driver. She was left with a traumatic brain injury that

---

2   Robbins, Anthony. *"Unleash the Power Within"*, 3/13/ 2021

impacted her quality of life. She used the two products I was introduced to with success. Three years and two months prior to the day Darlene approached me, my dad, my hero, had suffered a major neurological event that left him without 90 percent of his cerebellum. It was painful to see my dad living as he was. He experienced vertigo and nausea 24/7, had no sensation of hunger, and had to move his head to the left or right as painstakingly slow as possible. At the two-year anniversary, and despite his six hours of therapy a day, neurologists told us that my dad's brain had done all of the healing it could do.

To say that my father was skeptical when I told him that I wanted him to try a "replenishment product" is putting it lightly. He was angry that I had spent money on what could be "snake oil". If the neurologists couldn't help him, what could two products sold via NWM do? I only had to remind my dad about my diagnosis and ask him if he would do this for me. He opened his mind a tiny sliver to the possibilities and agreed.

Three-and-a-half days into taking this replenishment, my father explained that he, "...had an EPIPHANY"! When he opened his eyes, the world was spinning as usual, and then, the SPINNING JUST STOPPED!!! At first, he was fearful, and then, within minutes, he was like a new superhero testing out his powers. He spun around, looked up, down, left, and right and NO SPINNING, NO NAUSEA!!! All of those terrible effects from the neurological event were GONE! My dad got his life back on that night!!!

My conviction in the products and company started when my dad did a pirouette for me and my daughter the next morning! Our family felt elated, joyful, grateful, and hopeful! I began telling my dad's story, and pieces of a solution puzzle began falling into place.

As I stated earlier, dealing with cancer is a full-time job. Single-parenting is a full-time job. Navigating these two full-time jobs leaves few options for a paying full-time job (and would just lead me down the path that got me into this state of dysfunction in the first place). I needed something that I could fit into my life as it was. What could possibly fit into my schedule of single parenting, chemo treatments, physical therapy, surgeries, and co-parenting with a narcissist? What job would allow the ability to work when I felt good and the ability to listen to my body when needed? NWM would allow me all of this and much more.

As I progressed through my journey and added the two replenishments to my daily routine, I began to transform. I remember telling my therapist that I was feeling more joyful than I ever had in my life. What had changed was that I found HOPE in this company, these products, and in NWM. I found a solution for my and my daughter's needs. When I was given my diagnosis, I realized that the way that I was "living" before was not truly living. I was too exhausted and overworked to enjoy much. I vowed that I would never allow myself, ever again, to get into a position where my health was endangered, and that I would actually live life with my daughter. I have found my way, and I love helping others to find their way, too. NWM is hard work that requires consistency, thick skin, and a "why" that makes you cry. I am committed to doing what needs to be done, because I know what is possible.

What if Darlene listened to her inner self-limiting voice on that day and never shared with me about her company and products? What would my dad's life or my life look like? When your doubting thoughts about NWM creep in, will you remember my story and see NWM as I see it; as a gift? What's the worst that can happen when you invite someone to take a look at what you and your company have to offer? Even if they think you are "crazy", you will be able to rest your head easily on your pillow, as you shared and did not succumb to fear. What's the worst that can happen when you pass up an opportunity to share? The absolute worst is when someone tells me that they wish they knew about my products and company before their loved one passed. This is heart-breaking.

Once you choose the company, products, and leadership that align with your values and beliefs, go out there and be a BRAVE messenger. Be as BRAVE as the Paper Bag Princess when she confronted the dragon that kidnapped her prince and took away her earthly possessions[3]. Be prepared to leave those who are not yet ready to hear the message as the Paper Bag Princess left Prince Ronald, because he just "did not get it". Empower others to make their own choices by sharing this gift. Never prejudge. Consider your RIPPLE EFFECT, and help others to consider theirs. Go "teach many how to fish".

Thank you for your precious time in letting me share my story. I have an amazing team of people I work with who I adore and call my family. I visualize this family expanding every day throughout the world. If what I have expressed has resonated with you, connect with me on FB at: https://www.facebook.com/lisa.cassenti.9

 **Lisa Cassenti.** Lisa Cassenti is a single mom entrepreneur and breast cancer thriver. She received her BA in biology from SUNY at Stony Brook University in 1997. She studied capuchin monkeys in Argentina through SUNY at Stony Brook University, as her initial dream was to work in conservation biology with non-human primates. While applying to graduate school, she took a position working with teenagers with special needs. She fell in love with the children and the field of special education. She completed her student teaching at Bank Street and received her MA

---

3 Munsch, Robert. *The Paper Bag Princess*. Annick Press (U.S.) Ltd, 1980

in early childhood special education from Teachers College at Columbia University in 2001. Throughout her 24 years in special education, she worked with a primary concentration with children with autism. She worked primarily in early intervention (birth through three years) and CPSE (three through five years), supporting the children with special needs and their families in a variety of community settings. She then served as the Assistant Director for a NYC early intervention program for several years. At the end of 2018, she was diagnosed with breast cancer and found her way to health, hope, and happiness through being introduced to NWM. Her ripple effect is vast via her work in NWM. She adores partnering with single parents, advocates for patients of breast cancer, parents of children with special needs, those who love and work with animals, and female athletes.

www.lisacassenti.com.

CHAPTER 14

MOVING PEOPLE FORWARD IN BUSINESS AND LIFE
"BUSINESS IS AN INSIDE JOB"

Kim Pagano

I got my hair license when I was 18 and I bought a hair salon when I was 21. When I was finished with school, I signed up for a seminar. At this seminar, I learned a few great golden nuggets that I have carried with me throughout my career and I would like to share them with you. First, wherever you start in your industry is where you will finish. For example in my industry, I wanted to work for a high-end salon, so it would not serve me well to start in a small franchised salon because if I started building a clientele there they would not follow me. I thought it would ultimately be a waste of my time and effort. So in-stead I decided to go to the nicest salon I knew of to apply for a job, unbeknownst to me they were selling the salon and asked if want-ed to buy it. I learned early on to "fake it till you make it". I asked what that would look like, and that is when they told me the price was actually attainable to me. I was shocked, but if I would have said no and not seen the sign I would have missed out on the opportunity of owning my very own salon. The next step was to establish a business relationship with a bank so if I ever needed a loan or help in the future I would have a rapport with a bank. Fortunately, I didn't need a loan at the time as my dad lent me the money I needed, but the business relationship I built with the bank did come in handy later. I owned the salon for 15 years and I ended up becoming one of the top salons in that community. I also learned to dive in and learn how to swim, meaning I learned how to figure it all out. Building relationships with integrity was high on my list. I knew I had to be dependable and build the trust.

Soon after purchasing the salon my husband and I started a construction company. We pound-ed the pavement looking for opportunities and built our business from the ground up. I've learned that opportunities are everywhere, you just have to be open to the signs. Many years after being successful in hair I saw a small advertisement that said "Are you a mom with something to say?". I had no idea what that meant but it eventually opened another door. That was 16 years ago when I became a radio host of my own radio show. Again, that happened by watching for the signs. I had been doing hair for many years by this time and in my mind, I had already been interviewing my clients, so even though I had never done something like this before I had unknowingly been training for the next position in my life. Always look for the next signs in your path because that can take you to your next journey.

The next progression for me started showing up as clients and guests asked me to help them speak about their businesses in a powerful way. I have been doing this for all of my guests already, so again it was something that was easy for me. Supporting businesses is some-thing that I love. I have learned that it is my passion to help entrepreneurs find and live their dreams. I have also learned that how you run your business is usually how you run your life. I was taught early on that it is all in the consistency and the maintenance of the business. You can't just do it once and then leave and expect your business to run, it takes determination. You need to keep it maintained. Don't let things get overwhelming. If you need help look for someone that is qualified to help you. You also have to be coachable and be willing to try new things. Keep in touch with your clients. Make them feel important and needed. Collaborate with others to build your tribe. We as entrepreneurs must link arms, even more so during these uncertain times. We must focus on lifting and rising, building our community, and being a resource for anyone that might need it. If we are opening our hearts through business it will come full circle. My favorite saying is "many hands make little work". There are enough people to go around. Now is the time to shine the light on the brighter side of digital and social media for our businesses and our well beings. I have learned the importance of Zoom calls and learning new techniques. Brand yourself throughout social media. Say yes to things that present themselves to you even if you're afraid.

I heard an inspiring story from one of my guests many years ago on my radio show and it has always stuck with me. Pretend you are invited to a potluck dinner. What are you going to bring? Are you going to scrape together leftovers from the back of your refrigerator, or are you going to bring your best dish? This notion was intriguing and kept me exploring the question, "What does it mean to bring your best dish?". Bringing your best dish means bringing your best self wherever you go. Dress for success. It's not simply showing up for others at a specific place and time. It's having the respect to give them your full attention and being present for the people you are with and being mindful. Fake it until you make it, you are on stage. Bringing your best dish is bringing a positive, kind, and compassionate version of yourself to all dealings with others.

To bring your best dish consider the following steps:

Step 1: Do your best. You can't hit a home run if you don't step up to the plate. Decide to show up for people and for yourself. You don't have to be perfect. You don't have to get it right every time. Just do your best.

Step 2: Don't judge. Don't judge other people and don't judge yourself. You are unique and have something special to offer - remember to treat yourself that way.

Step 3: No regrets. We often beat ourselves up for what we didn't do, what we didn't say, or for any kindness that we failed to offer. There is no need to live in the past, or the future. All we have is the present. Rather than regretting what you might have done imperfectly, focus on ways that you can bring your best self forward now.

Ultimately, bringing your best offers the greatest opportunities for connection, getting what you need, giving to others, and experiencing joy in life. Since all opportunities come through people, everyone benefits when you put your best self forward. Running your business is a lot like building. You start by being clear with your vision and making sure you have all of your facts correct, and ensuring that this can be done the way you believed it could. Then, you get all of your permits and everything approved so you can start on the foundation. By following these important steps, everyone wins in the end.

 **Kim Pagano** is a wife and a mother of four, and so much more Kim's newest treasure is her grandchildren.. She is very close with her family. She is involved in her community and supports several non profits that are dear to her heart. Kim has been a Hair Therapist for years. Kim's passion is making people look good from the outside in. Kim's theory is Look good, feel good Do great!

Kim & her husband joined forces many years ago by starting their Construction Company. She loves entertaining, her roses. ! She has recently been following her passions, which has led her to the next chapter in her life, hosting "Kim Pagano Show, Positive Talk Radio", being the Voice for Women everywhere and making great connections. Kim Pagano is the host of the Kim Pagano Radio Show, brought to you by the award winning talk radio station 1590 KVTA. Kim brings you " Guests from all over the world"

Kim has also created her own Women's Support Group, where she not only gets women together, but also focuses on positive topics that are near and dear to their hearts, making quality relationships to grow on. Kim has also started coaching entrepreneurs to be able to speak their business ,so they can get their message across in a powerful way. Kim's favorite saying is "Fake it till you make it" and it works Kim firmly believes that "many hands make little work" the more people involved in any project the easier it should be. Kim is a very passionate lady who keeps so many things close to her heart.

www.kimpaganoshow.com

CHAPTER 15

WORDS MATTER

Bud Ayers

Hi! My name is Bud Ayers. I am a lecturer, author, speaker, dancer, and entrepreneur. I am part owner of a network marketing company called Bonvera, as well as a member of the Ibuumerang Organization.

I am sure you have heard it all before. "Change your thinking, change your life." And you ask, "But where do I start?"

By simply changing the word "need" to "want", you will see a major change in your life. But first, we have to look at your thinking. Thinking is the most important thing to change when it comes to improving our lives. Here are my two favorite quotes on the subject.

"We cannot solve our problems with the same thinking we used when we created Them." – Albert Einstein

"Thinking is one of the hardest things for a man to do. That's why so few do it." –Henry Ford

I would like you to pay attention to how many times you say the word "need" on a daily basis. Become aware and count them in a day. Once you are able to identify how often you say it, make a note to see whether or not that need has been taken care of. Let me give you a few examples.

I need to stop procrastinating.

I need to get my taxes done.

I need to lose weight.

I need to make more money.

I need to get a job.

I need someone in my life.

I need to quit smoking.

I want you to notice or pay attention to how you feel when you say it. Do you feel like you're in control? Do you feel like you powerless to do it? Do you feel like it will get done when you want it to be done? Let's try changing one word and see what effect it has.

I want to stop procrastinating.

I want to get my taxes done.

I want to lose weight.

I want to make more money.

I want to get a job.

I want someone in my life.

I want to quit smoking.

Did you feel different when you used the word "want" instead of "need"? What I have found is many people use the word "need" when they really don't want to do something. And the result is, it doesn't get done. "Needing to" are words of the powerless.

Pay attention to how many times politicians say, "We need this, or we need that."

Notice that we don't get most of those things.

A favorite example I like to use is the old Uncle Sam poster. "Uncle Sam wants you." He doesn't need you. Better yet, you see help wanted signs, not help needed signs.

The brain hears the word "need" and immediately interprets it as you are not in charge or capable of achieving it. When we use the word "want", we subconsciously tell ourselves "I deserve this."

To demonstrate my point. Ask yourself these questions:

Do you need a new career?

Do you want a new career?

Do you need a new car?

Do you want a new car?

Do you need to be in a relationship?

Do you want to be in a relationship?

You soon get the picture of the difference between needing to and wanting to.

NEED stands for:

Nothing

Ever

Ever

Develops

You will never see a poster that says "forget the needy - feed the greedy". Needy people don't get, because they don't feel they have the power to receive; whereas, greedy people take or get because they want it. To be clear, I am not advocating greed; I am simply saying that their state of mind is very different from someone who is needy.

For me, WANT means:

Will		Will
Apply	Or	Attract
New		New
Thinking		Things

As I have mentioned earlier, almost everything that happens to us in our life is based on our thinking. People are successful because of the way they think and act.

Not all rich people got there through hard work; some people get there through luck or connections and even illegal means, but that is not our focus.

In my opinion, there are only five things in life that you need, and without these things you die: air, sleep, water, food, and love. Here is an easy way to remember them:

FLAWS: Food, love, air, water, and sleep

Everything else (yes, including housing and clothing) is a want.

Mindset, Habit, And Education

How many of you have been told, "Go to school, get good grades, get a degree, and get a good job." Here is the thing…it is no longer feasible. The truth is, many businesses only focus on their bottom line. In our parents' or grandparents' days, businesses provided pensions and took care of their long-term employees.

Reductions and changes in regulations have allowed many businesses to eliminate that practice. Many will even pay you a bonus, as opposed to retirement benefits. If a business doesn't make a profit, there will be no business. Remember, the purpose of a business is to make money, not create jobs. Jobs are offered when the workload is too great for a person to do, but believe me, most successful businesses will squeeze every cent out of their workforce. That's why some businesses start with good pay and normal hours and eventually increase the workload until you end up actually working for less and less money. Here is an example.

Let's say you make $10K a month for 40 hours a week. Good right? Let's say the workload now increased to 48 hours a week or nine to ten hours a day. Your pay just got cut by 20 percent. If you eventually start to work 60 hours a week, you are now getting a 50 percent cut in pay. They get you in the front door, but then, eventually, it becomes your prison. In addition, many businesses now outsource their work force.

Point being, it is no longer your education but your habits and mindset that will determine your success. If a college education degree is the key to success, why do 60 percent of college graduates get jobs that are not related to their education?

This is also why entrepreneurship is so important. It gives you the ability to control your own destiny.

Here are a few books that I recommend reading to develop a winning mindset:

Secrets of a Millionaire Mind, by T. Harv Eker

7 Habits of Highly Effective People, by Stephen Covey

Underdog Millionaire, by J.T. Foxx

Notice, not a single book talks about education. It's not education; it's mindset that will get you ahead. Education gives you knowledge, but not experience. Formal education gives you a degree, but not leadership skills. Formal education does not teach you communication skills. Formal education does not teach how to overcome obstacles. Formal education does not teach you sales, problem solving, and success development skills. These are skills that will make you successful in any kind of business, whether working for someone else, or for yourself as you enter the world of entrepreneurship.

I have shared this information with thousands of people, and many have thanked me for helping them realize how their mindset limited them and changed the results in their lives.

I hope in the end, that you stop "needing to" and start "wanting to". One final piece of advice. Be kind to yourself. No one is perfect. I have found that life is more interesting with its up and downs. The difference between walking through a hilly path rather than a flat desert is that the hills allow you to get a different perspective. You are always with your thoughts, and the world is already filled with people who will judge you for every little thing. It's okay to be down once in a while. Just don't stay there too long.

I leave you with this quote by Mahatma Ghandi

Keep your thoughts positive
Because your thoughts become
YOUR WORDS

Keep your words positive
Because your words become
YOUR BEHAVIOR

Keep your behavior positive
Because your behavior becomes
YOUR HABITS

Keep your habits positive
Because your habits become
YOUR VALUES

Keep your values positive
Because your values become
YOUR DESTINY

Albert "Bud" Ayers is an author, speaker, lecturer, entrepreneur, producer, choreographer and ballroom dancer.

Bud helps you understand that there is more to life than a college degree. He encourages you to step out of your comfort zone and take more risks by becoming entrepreneurs.

His varied experiences in manufacturing, distribution, personal growth, sports, communication, entertainment, entrepreneur, public speaking and ballroom dancing give him a unique supply of resources, and perspective.

He wants to share his life experiences with you with the hope that the lessons he teaches will help you navigate the challenges of life.

His words of wisdom guarantees that you will be a different person if you apply the knowledge that he shares in your life. He informs you that you have the power to change anything in your life by changing their choices of words you say to yourself. This is the inspiration for his book "Words Matter"

He inspires you to take risks, accept failure and be better at communication and becoming a forceforgood. He believes that knowledge is simply a too land must be applied before it can become expertise

He is known for his passion in sharing his wisdom and helping you navigate your personal challenges in finding success and happiness.

He is happily married and has three children and 7 grandchildren.
www.WordsMatterbyBudAyers.com

CHAPTER 16

YOU SHOULD READ THIS

Mary Dee

"First forget inspiration. Habit is more dependable.
Habit will sustain you whether you're inspired or not."
-Octavia Butler

I have many amazing friends and professionals I know from all of my years in the industry and one thing that stands out the most is their level of consistency and focus. They stayed the course, they worked their system and they were always adding value to their teams. They created consistent habits that led to consistent results. They researched an opportunity before they jumped in and they made sure the opportunity aligned with their goals and values. Once there was alignment, they weren't distracted by every shiny ball and every other opportunity lingering out in the world.

When you can line up your personal core values with your company you'll find that your "why" will be strong and harmonious. You are going to need that "why," that big reason, to get you through some days. It's easy to get caught up in the administrative time sucks of the day to day business which is why staying consistent and doing those activities that generate income and nurture relationships are where you want to spend the majority of your time every day. Get sticky. Stick to your business, stick to your products, stick to your results, stick to your team and stick to your message. Stickiness is what will keep your customers, potential customers and downline around long enough to be life long customers and life long friends.

If you are struggling with shiny ball syndrome or lack of motivation that's typically a sign that the conviction behind your "why" simply isn't important enough. There's a great framework for really getting to your why to create accountability to yourself for your dreams.

Motivation tends to increase not because we are waiting for something to peel us up off the couch and do it, but rather when we make an intentional decision to do the task- once we're in it motivation happens as a side effect. I would encourage you to write down WHAT you're trying to get motivated to do (i.e. 100 push ups) but go a level deeper and and write down WHY you want it (i.e. You want toned arms). Then keep writing down another layer deep of WHY (i.e. Weight bearing exercise is good for me also...) By the time you get to about the 5th WHY the real reason behind what you want should reveal itself (i.e. I want do do push ups because I believe they are a good exercise that will be healthy for my body because I want to live as long as possible).

Once you're super clear on that process, it's time to set yourself up for success through accountability.

Once you know why- accountability is best served up warm with a side of good habits.

At the end of 2017 I was diagnosed with breast cancer and for over 2 weeks I had to wait to see a specialist before they would actually explain what that meant and what my options were for treatment. I battled back and forth in my mind as to whether I was going to get a stage 0- you're going to be fine diagnosis or a stage 4- get your affairs in order diagnosis. Many days were a struggle to even get out of bed because I had so much uncertainty about the future. I was feeling overwhelmed and lost.

One thing that held me through not just those 2 weeks but also throughout the years to follow- were my good habits. Habits can be fun and interesting, they are not required to be rigid and boring! While some people will sit around waiting to get motivated, you can actually *activate* motivation by creating habits that support the goal you have in mind.

Design a wake-up and wind-down routine* that will ground you and give you a purpose so that on days where you're not feeling motivated and not feeling purposeful, you still make time to create intentional space for what matters most.

Neither routine has to be a certain length of time. Some of my best mentors over the years take the first 2 hours of their day just for them. This is the time they use to work out, pray, meditate, read or spend time on their wellness or personal development.

Mine looks something like this...wake up to my favorite playlist and lay in bed for the first couple of songs stretching and creating small movements while I speak an intention and gratitude into my new day. I drink 24 warm ounces of Himalyan pink salt water to rehydrate my body. After that I invest in a little strength training, some dips, push ups, squats and more stretching. I dance around and really feel the music in my cells, say a little prayer and bless the day. Then I get ready to dive into my day.

This morning routine for me is simple but it's really effective. Some days it takes me an hour to do the ritual. Other times I do it in 15 minutes. Find the ritual that kicks off your day with joy and it will guarantee you a morning of delight. No matter how crazy my day might be, my wake-up routine ensures that I get in very intentional time for my mental and physical health before I ever fully step into the day.

A wind-down routine allows you to close the day intentionally- taking time to bless the day for it's lessons and wins, but also to close the book on that day so that you don't take it with you to bed. Once you have reflected on the day and closed it out, the ritual begins. The evening is a beautiful time to indulge in personal development and self-care. Your mind will actually be able to recognize your routines before bed and that allows your body to prepare for rest and repair.

For my wind down routine I love to take a shower, apply my different creams and lotions, enjoy some easy listening tunes, drink a warm cup of herbal tea, read a book, journal, pray and then end my day speaking gratitudes until I fall asleep. I haven't had a bad dream in years and I'm pretty sure this routine has influenced those results greatly.

Amazing habits can not only enhance your life by their grounding effects but also they are the framework for creating any other results you may be trying to achieve. The wake-up and wind-down routines are wonderful to ground you and create purposeful movement and activity before a day starts and before it ends. Think of every day like a book-knowing that you can write a new story for your life every day!

Mary Dee. Known as "The Joy Catalyst" Mary Dee is an International Speaker, Best Selling Author and trusted Business Advisor at the MADLOVE Agency. She's been advising for over 20 years, playing predominantly in the network marketing, influencer and agency spaces, to help impact driven businesses create a winning strategy and culture. She's built multiple start-ups from an idea into a multi-million dollar enterprise.

Mary is sought after for her sage advice, love heartedness and ability to foster a safe environment that promotes discovery, growth and breakthroughs. Her signature program, **Madloveology** is designed to help you transform your pain into passion so that you can fall in love with your life again. She'll show you how to say no to the grind and say yes to abundance through 8 key frameworks that are guaranteed to create lasting results in your life so you can have the freedom, peace and life that you crave.

In 2018 Mary healed from Breast Cancer holistically after surgery and she helps those on their own journey with cancer stay encouraged and empowered to make decisions based on faith and not fear. She's Chair of the Board for thebreasties.org, a 501(c)(3) community that supports young women affected by breast cancer with resources, encouragement and connection. She's available for speaking engagements, mentorship and adventure. For more great stories, inspiration and magic mindset moments, head over to www.marydee.com or join her on Instagram, Facebook & Clubhouse @themarydee

www.marydee.com

CHAPTER 17

WHAT IS THE NEXT LEVEL OF OUR SHIFTING WORLD?

Daniel Bolin

What is the next level of our shifting world? It is my desire to create a new way of being human with our world thriving through a wisdom-sharing-based economy! How I stumbled through network marketing as a way to change my health in 1993 with a company called Herbalife. The initial success with Herbalife and what awoke me to the thought continuing the network marketing journey.

Fast forward, to this now moment, being a wealth of knowledge engaged in network marketing in many forms for 28 years, and it has been the sweetest road to enlightenment and inner reflection on self and the hero's journey. I really started to know my inner being and limitations because of my drives and desires to help others obtain the levels of success and enjoyment of moving into a wisdom-based, passion-driven, home-based lifestyle.

You see, I was introduced to network marketing at the young age of 19, and I saw it as a way to get amazing products that were very expensive sent to my home monthly for the cost of shipping. Way back then, we did not have the Internet, and it was a very person-to-person driven business. I quickly found out that many of my friends did not have the courage or curiosity to learn how to speak to others and share their story or believe in the community-based direct sales model.

So, a major pitfall of network marketing fell upon me very quickly, as my friends and family informed me they could no longer continue to pay the high cost of these supplements, and they found cheaper alternatives or gave up on the possibility of creating a side hustle. It is very easy to place the blame of lack of success on many other factors other than myself, and I have heard of and done most of these shift-the-blame victim mentality games myself.

On the other hand, I was busy staying positive and finding all the blessings and the reasons why I could continue to pay for the best products when I no longer had three referrals continuing to get my products for free. One of my earliest gifts given to me from a mentor in sales was to always be a product of the product and only work with the best. Never sell something you do not see the value in, because without true passion, sales will be difficult, due to the fact that it would harm your own personal beliefs and self-esteem.

An exciting belief came because of the tax burden pains I felt as I paid my first taxes and I learned of being in the highest tax bracket of a W-2 wage earner. When I received my first tax return, I was incredibly discouraged by the amount of taxes taken from me when I claimed zero dependents and expected a nice return, but outraged when it was just a little over $100 dollars. Being incredibly upset by this outcome, I quickly learned through having my home-based business and getting a tax accountant that my home-based business increased my next year's return to $2,000.

That easily paid for my year's supply of products and got me very excited about having money that I was not attached to additional I would never have acquired without gaining knowledge of without learning about the benefits of business ownership.. I saw that potential as a powerful potential to a better life and not following in the footsteps of living paycheck to paycheck, like so many people I knew.

My accountant then gave me additional tips and ways to recoup more lost dollars and jumped into a mindset of knowing it wasn't about how much you make, but how much you can keep. In the next tax season, I received $4,300 back in tax returns, followed by $7,200 the next year. These financial concepts allowed me to afford a dream vacation and new beliefs in my money mindset to invest in my business and myself that shifted my idea of network marketing to always having a bigger dream and to keep working towards better.

Although there was a caveat to being attached to this new focus, as I was able to hide my lack of finding others and training them to have the success and excitement that I was having that limited my growth as a leader. The inner story I was telling myself that I was mostly unaware of shifted my focus dramatically, and my shadow started to grow like a veil to cover my fears of not being enough. The internal conflict began to change my beliefs of what was possible, and I started playing small and avoiding parts of growing my skills that altered my business success. Those inner beliefs were controlling me in the background, but I was unaware, and I continued on my journey of denying it was my fault and going from one shiny object to the next in the network marketing game.

One blessing was that I did continue on the path of self-development, and I went to many seminars and continued to acquire knowledge and grow my network, meet all types of personalities, and travel the United States. There are so many facets of network marketing, business development, and self-development that it can be a very difficult balance, which can lead to fragmentation of your thoughts and confidence.

One of the most powerful tools to my transformation was to break free of my self-limiting thoughts and beliefs by acknowledging the power of my shadow. The shadow is a way of describing the secretive hidden trickster voices in your head that are affecting all of your decisions and relationships. When we examine the random thought energy of the mind, we can take a deep dive into our inner mindset and understand the multiple levels of self that subconsciously control most of our lives through unseen non-logic-based choices to life's resistance to change.

Your primal self has a goal to keep you safe from harm and these traumas that were placed upon you in your young life will have automatic emotional reactions to protect you and will always be the worst-case scenario until you take the time to retrain your reactive mind. Ask your inner self the hard questions, and then, find the courage to ask better questions of yourself that will allow the creative mind to come up with better solutions. It is important to understand the role of your inner dialogue. To acknowledge your inner child and your inner critic, as they are always in battle or conflict, then shift your focus and power to create your life.

The hero's journey is one to correct or get in touch with and know "I can overcome this societal form of control or mental enslavement." We see representations of the shadow battle displayed in cartoons, movies, music, and, of course, the holy books. Some of the classic examples of this duality are the angel and the devil on our shoulders, the light and the darkness, the head and the heart, the hero and the victim, and the yin and the yang.

You can break free. The choice has always been yours and yours alone. No one can get into your beautiful mind and drive for you. That is a deep dive into the inner self that you must have the courage to continue to revisit as you unfold your layers and remove the veils of your perception that have been clouding your vision.

I may share the many stories and levels of my journey, but no one can take the steps you require. I can and will walk beside you as a guide.

"Don't walk beside me; I may not lead.

Don't watch in front of me; I may not follow.

Just walk beside me and be my friend." ~ Author unknown

I have been getting reacquainted with my intuitive nature as a result of exploring multi-level sales. It is a blessed road to unconditional love of self-leadership (development). I'm going to go outside of the norm to reclaim my joy, showing my willingness to be my true authentic self, to share what I believe in and feel strongly about when I speak divinely to others. In the unconditional love of my daughter, I've been able to see the feminine side in myself.

Speaking through my heart and the burning desire to reconnect with my child self, to give permission to be curious and choose my words carefully as I would like my daughter, my loved ones to see the world through unfiltered joyful eyes. To witness magical healing transformations as I am thankful for those beautiful blessings that feel so wonderful, to know true tears of joy.

I really feel your energy, your struggles, and your compassion. Thank you. I appreciate your energy and time, first and foremost. I am humbled to be invited to share my path; it is a cherished honor.

 **Daniel Bolin** knows first-hand the overwhelm and frustration of self-limiting intrusive thoughts sabotaging our inner happiness and spark for life. He has reconnected with the inner enlightened spiritual being who possesses unconditional love, positivity, kindness, and true compassion. Bolin has his own business, where he works one-on-one with his clients, helping them recognize within this beautiful way of being calm and influencing ourselves to reach higher.

Shifting focus channeling our natural energy to promote healing the relationship with self by recognizing the mind-body connection. The body communicates our deepest needs.

Interacting with others with the intention of improving their life without expectations. Bolin guides, shares, and takes action to show ourselves compassion when we are in turmoil or confusion. He helps identify the unseen subconscious obstacles that get in the way of happy day-to-day living and enables us to withdraw from negative energy patterns of pain that block us from healing the wounds that are continually keeping us from achieving our best life. Bolin's gift is sharing self-awareness in a way that's heartfelt, to dive deep within, and help others rediscover their true passions.

Bolin is most active on Facebook, where he shares his inner work (journey) freely, without anxiety or expectations. He openly shares his dark past to help others appreciate that we are not alone in our struggles, and we are, in fact, in this together, to gain true power rebuilding our tribes. Bolin is firm in his beliefs and own inner understanding of life's deeper purpose, yet kind and compassionate with his message.

www.empoweredrockstar.com

CHAPTER 18

FOLLOW YOUR GUT

Laura Klein

In 1985, I was a college graduate, newly married, with a large amount of school loan debt. My husband and I decided to enlist in the Army National Guard to pay off our college loans. The requirement of one weekend a month, and a few weeks of training seemed manageable. I had no idea that this decision would not only change the trajectory of my life; but among other things, who I would become as a mother, a teacher, an entrepreneur, and a leader.

I graduated from Basic Training and started my journey as a "weekend warrior". A few years later, I attended Officer Candidate School and earned my "gold bar" as a Second Lieutenant. It was this experience that commenced my leadership journey that would serve me for years to come.

During my tenure in the "guard", and teaching children with special needs full time, I was blessed with two little girls. I knew it was time to hang up my army boots and enter the Inactive Ready Reserves. Within months, stories of turmoil brewing in the Middle East made headline news. I was relieved that I had completed my required enlistment and felt "safe" in the Inactive Ready Reserve.

December 10. A day I will never forget for as long as I live. I received a phone call from my company commander, who informed me that I needed to report to active duty within 24 hours. I immediately assumed that there must be a mistake! My daughters were just two years old and three weeks old. After the call ended, I became physically ill. I stayed up all night, staring at my babies while they slept. Would I be in danger? Would I ever see them again? I felt a total sense of abandonment. I would have taken those hefty college loans back in an instant.

We arrived in Saudi Arabia in January 1991. My naivety of what I thought I might see and experience was dismissed in a flash. The air strip was surrounded by patriot missile systems to protect the incoming troops and critical cargo. We were quickly transported to soldier barracks within miles of the airport. The buildings had been bombed repeatedly and many were damaged beyond repair. Within hours, our welcoming committee, the "enemy", decided to make their presence known by directing scud missiles in our direction. My platoon and I were huddled in a tiny room in complete darkness while warning sirens vibrated the thin walls. Putting our extensive training into action, we immediately donned our gas masks for protection. Amid the chaos, one of my soldiers experienced a panic attack and refused to put on his protective gear. This was truly my first experience as a leader under duress. I have always believed that leadership is influence, but in this instant, there was no time for a conversation on compliance. We physically restrained him and put the protective mask on him. My first lesson in leadership in a war zone reinforced the notion that those we lead, especially in times of great stress and fear, really watch and model our behavior. I thought we might die that night, but I remained calm, and it paid off. The missiles never hit their target, and we survived our first night.

Our military police mission in Saudi Arabia was to oversee a POW camp that guarded Iraqi refugees and Republican Guard soldiers. In my downtime, I'd sit on a sand dune overlooking the vast desert. This time alone allowed me to have many "bargaining" conversations with God. If I make it home, I will live my best life. If I am reunited with my children, I will do whatever it takes to create the ideal life for them. For years, I had allowed myself to settle in a toxic relationship. It's interesting how strong and resilient you become when faced with mortality. The clarity I gained during these moments of self-reflection were huge.

Looking back, we were extremely fortunate. Kuwait was liberated quickly, and we returned home in five short months, even though it felt like five long years. Soon after my return, I filed for divorce and began my new journey of self-sufficiency and self-discovery. It wasn't easy; but, nothing truly transformational ever is.

I returned to the classroom as a junior high school teacher, where I struggled financially as a single mom. I acquired cash advances on my credit cards to pay for daycare and buy groceries. Pursuing child support proved to be a waste of time and money. Relying on someone "unpredictable" and "disengaged" to support my children petrified me, and I knew I had to devise a plan of action that would secure our financial future.

I decided to do what most people would consider a safe bet. I enrolled into a local university to pursue a Master's degree in educational administration. Once I graduated, I took a whopping $50 a month pay increase. To earn a significant pay raise, I would have to secure a position as a school administrator that would require about 60 to 70 hours a week. After my military deployment, I decided that I would never again spend extended periods of time away from my girls.

In the summer of 1993, one of my best friends reached out and offered me an opportunity to start a direct sales business. I asked her if I could make an extra $500 per month, and she thought that I could. Okay…I'm in. After attending a national conference with this company, I soon realized that I had found my niche. I was going to build BIG, be on that national stage as a top performer, and earn life-changing income.

However, to my disappointment, no one in my immediate circle of family and friends bought a ticket on the same train I was on.

I shared my vision of leaving my teaching career with my colleagues in the teacher's lounge. They said I was crazy. My uncle, a successful businessman who I admired, advised me to stick to teaching. The man I started dating, who is now my awesome husband of 25 years, was concerned that I was taking on a second job. I knew the advice I received came from a place of love and concern. And honestly, it's just the way we've been wired to think in our society. Go to college, get a good job, work in this capacity for 30 years or more and retire. There's nothing wrong with that course of action; but for me, it wasn't going to serve my dreams and ambitions any longer.

I followed my gut. I realized that I didn't need anyone's blessing or permission to take that leap of faith. I accepted 100 percent responsibility for my choices and committed to succeeding. My life's experiences by age 30 had helped me transform from a self-doubting, insecure person to a visionary leader who saw unlimited potential. Adversity was the catalyst that drove me to defy the limits that traditional career choices presented to me. It was time to live my best life, show others how to do it, and never accept mediocrity ever again.

I went on to build a large organization in my first company, earning an amazing income seven times my teacher salary. The monetary rewards were life-changing. I could mention all the other incentives that I've received from my career in direct sales, but the reality is that money allows you to change your circumstances, and, if you make enough of it, you can change other people's circumstances as well.

In 2013, after 20 years with my first direct sales company, I decided to pursue a career with another company that mirrored the same business model. On this new journey, I surrounded myself with amazing people and built to a top executive rank in five short months. That's just one of the benefits of this chosen profession: once you learn the skill set of selling and building teams, and have the proper systems in place, you can experience success just about anywhere you want to go!

Undoubtedly, these last eighteen months have presented unforeseen challenges to every business in the United States on so many levels. It was during these uncertain times that I started to consider retirement. In my 28-year tenure, I've experienced the ups and downs of our economy and horrific national tragedies: the UPS strike in 1997, 9/11, the economic collapse in 2008, and now, a virus that has rendered one-third of all small businesses in the United States non-operational. Obstacles come and go, but the opportunity in network marketing remains constant, patiently waiting on us to work through difficult times.

Despite inching closer to retirement age as defined by the traditional career sector, I concluded in the end that I'll never leave this amazing industry. What I love about network marketing is that this profession doesn't discriminate based on gender, age, or any other demographic. A career in network marketing is for anyone at any time willing to work the program.

My advice is simple: break the mold. Defy the status quo. Politely listen to nay-sayers. Follow your dreams anyway. Treat it like a profession. Create a vision. Influence others. Work hard. Work harder. Navigate around, over, and under all obstacles. Never, ever give up. And always follow your gut.

 **Laura Klein** is the founder of Laura Klein Group—a business consulting and training group specializing in working with women business owners, and entrepreneurs. Laura Klein Group's training programs address enhancing leadership skills, increasing effective communications, implementing growth strategies, and teaching new ways of doing business in the 21st century. In addition, she is also a certified John Maxwell coach.

Klein spent 28 years as a senior executive with two separate direct sales companies, working extensively with independent contractors to promote increased sales and team building. Within that 28-year tenure, Klein joined a new direct sales company in 2013, where she climbed to the top ranks of Senior Director in five short months, earning a trip to Austria & Switzerland and a BMW of her choice. In eight short years, her total organizational sales exceeded 4.7 million! Her current team consists of over 1,000 consultants and leaders across the U.S., from California to Maine.

Other awards she has received include BNI Mid America's All-Star Award for being an exceptional chapter member and in 2019, "Business Person of the Year" from Southwestern Illinois Small Business Week. She also received exclusive awards during her time in the military to include Top Officer of the Cycle during her training at Officer Candidate School. After her tour of duty in Saudi Arabia, she was awarded the Medal of Accommodation, Southwest Asia Service Medal, and the Kuwait Liberation Medal.

Klein has been married to her husband, Doug, for 25 years, and they are the proud parents of a blended family of five adult children! Her and Doug have five grandchildren, and ten grand dogs.

When Klein is not consulting, speaking, or training, she donates her time to non-for-profits that she is passionate about: NAMI (National

Alliance on Mental Illness), Stray Rescue of St. Louis, the Belleville Humane Society, and the American Cancer Society. She also serves on the Board of Directors with Feed My People, St. Louis. When time allows, you can find her strategizing in her kitchen, cooking up home-made meals so that her children and grandchildren have a reason to visit. She believes that the best memories are made around the table!

Klein's favorite quote: When you get tired, rest; but never quit.

www.laurakleingroup.com

CHAPTER 19

ECONOMICS OF ABUNDANCE:
BIBLICAL PRINCIPLES TO LIVE YOUR PASSION ON PURPOSE

Sharon Salvador , MBA

The following testimony shares landmark periods of time in my life where God brought me to a point of demarcation. The changes were dramatic and His influence undeniable as my true purpose was revealed. I can now live intentionally with a sense of purpose to better navigate life's challenges and enjoy His blessings daily.

Points of Demarcation

Not pleased with low-self esteem, praying silent prayers believing I was unworthy of the blessings God had in store for me, fearing the supernatural force I knew was looking for me to surrender all to the Lord – I sought to understand why. The result: low revelation, lacking in intimacy with the Lord, and allowing the enemy to prey on my mind with doubts that clouded my sensitivity to the Lord's presence.

At the age of 24, after a serious car accident that left me unable to work, succeeded six weeks later by my father's death, I was left freefalling in an emotional abyss. All the resentment I felt towards my absentee father and the remorse provoked was like a ton of bricks worth of guilt crushing my spirit. Through the physical therapy, the support of my family and a few friends, God showed His mercy on me. He poured

Himself into me, and needless to say, I had to change my priorities. He saved me from my fall to hell as I cried out to Jesus, and I woke up from that vision to another level of awareness.

He heals me from the emotional turmoil and brings a new perspective of the new person I was to be. He led me to His word and shone light on what my new profession would be. By this point, I had been a part-time freelance consultant, but from that point forward, I would not work for a formal institution as an employee. After two years of physical and emotional therapy, I thought I was healed but still went back to old bad habits – not going to church, not reading the Bible regularly, and of course, not praying effective prayers. I found myself, sadly, not giving God His proper place in my life.

And still…He continues to love me by blessing me with sustenance and blessing my business with financial overflow that allowed me to be of blessings to others. The Lord allowed for me to be a breadwinner in my household (supporting myself, my family, and my new business). Despite all the blessings, I still had doubts from lack of knowledge in the Word and a flailing faith walk. How ungrateful was I?

This doubt perpetuated disbelief, a skewed perception of self that resulted in an underlying sadness, frustration, and dissatisfaction with the portrayal of the happy mask I wore on a daily basis. I wondered: where had I gone wrong? Why do I still crave direction in my life, as though I was not already found? Why do I fear being close to God? I've known Him all my life—or so I thought.

I can list a litany of where I thought I went wrong, how I knew I was living outside of the will of God, all my shortcomings and what I *thought* I was doing wrong (not consecrating myself to the Lord, not congregating or fellowshipping with other Christians, delving into the darkness of my barrage of negative thoughts, not reading the Bible consistently, and so on).

Though I know God has been working on me and was with me my entire life, I can pinpoint yet another marked point of demarcation in my faith walk – congregating and finding a church home.

Indeed, He makes all things new, and He is faithful. "…For he is faithful to do what he says…"(1

Corinthians 1:9).

The Lord led me there subtly, but His impact was evident. I felt the warmth of God's embrace I so craved – another prayer answered. This felt like the renewal my faith walk sought for ten years. Things that took precedence over God were revealed to me. I broke ties with many people, and most of all my self-loathing, pessimistic, problem-identifying mindset.

I now felt like a participant in life, and the decision to once again fellowship with the Lord was made – leaving behind all religiosity, meaningless rituals, and finally seeking the Lord through a heart of surrender. Finally depending on Him like I should have all along.

The intimacy I craved in my personal relationships is the intimacy I now know I should have been seeking with Him. The enemy and I knew this was my weakness. Despite knowing this, I felt powerless to make any changes.

Power of Prayer

Once learning the true purpose of prayer, releasing the fear of the spiritual realm and grasping the grace He has bestowed upon my life, I am now empowered beyond my comfort zone to simply be a vessel of the release of His will here, on Earth. How powerful is that!

To know your true identity and be in harmony with how God views you is beyond compare. No longer seeking earthly-bound conceptions of who you are or should be is nothing less than amazing!

The analogy of being an ambassador of Heaven spoke deep to my heart, as I truly believe this has been my true life's purpose. It awakened and confirmed my belief in this truth. I finally felt the call He had been preparing me for my entire life. Knowing my role in heaven clarified further what my role here, on Earth, actually is. Having my clarity of purpose crystalized gave me the focus and discipline I needed to have in my faith walk, hence, giving me the direction I so desperately needed to prioritize my daily goals accordingly.

This truth has allowed me to finally have the courage to speak up against the enemy's works (negative thoughts) out loud and not be concerned with onlookers' perception of me. To realize the great courage that Jesus possessed inspired me to have courage to at least speak His words and own the power His name releases when spoken.

Without fear of retribution, I can better commune with the Lord throughout the day; I can now say that I have a strategy in my prayers. No longer speaking in general terms, but in specific, Bible-founded words, as I seek His presence daily. I can now say I have a strategy to create, call into existence and wield this powerful weapon to defeat the enemy's attacks. I am bold enough to pray confidently any time.

Confirmation of New Direction

In the past, I felt like a fledgling Christian, begging for morsels of faith to get through the day – not realizing the great power the Lord has bestowed on me, containing the untapped potential brewing just outside my reach. With an improved self-esteem, I find myself working the power poured into me – unafraid to call on His Name, to depend on Him, and not my own efforts.

"Our position as believers in Christ gives us a legal right to pray in the Name of Jesus and take out of that Name the wealth of love, and riches, and grace, and salvation, and redemption that belongs to us" (Kenyon, 2012).

In God's true form, He shows His love and repeats Himself until I understand (as if I needed further confirmation!) that I was still a fledgling then.

We believers need to change our ways and mature spiritually by activating our faith as we continue to seek Him and His kingdom. The message, centered on Luke 5, spoke of Peter's call to transform his profession as fisher of fish to a fisher of men, how we are to live Jesus' teachings, digest the Word, and take action. Faith is made active through actions, changes in behavior, and ultimately being the Heavenly representatives we are designed to be.

We must assume our rightful role and follow God's calling to be disciples, to be a fisher of men, to be in communion with Him, and to use Jesus as our role model. Above all else, to have total faith in Him and accept the grace and rewards He has granted us.

New Focus

After over 20 years as a business consultant, the Lord inspires me to trade my profession for His calling. My personal and business focus has transformed yet again.

First is to be an ambassador of Heaven. I shall continue formal study of the Word of God and use my business acumen for God's purposes of sharing the Good News. He's even introduced new Christian business ventures already! I am excited about living out the new adventures He has set forth before me.

If my memory fails, to yet again forget whom I belong to, whom I want to please (John 5:30), I just need to remember I am His child who bears her Savior's name…(Salvador = "Savior" in Spanish)! ☺

 **Sharon Salvador MBA.** Sharon Salvador is a Dominican-American woman, raised and educated in Newark, New Jersey, who at 15 years old became an active and conscious community activist compelled to support community-based organizations in affecting the disaffected. A first generation graduate with a bachelor's degree in economics from Rutgers University and an MBA from University of Phoenix, she formalized her consulting business and serves the community at large in a multitude of endeavors.

Financial education is the core of her personal service platform. As she strives to be an example, in her family and community, now is the most opportune time to share resources about a subject matter at the center of quality-of-life improvement for the masses. Salvador always seeks to make a greater positive impact.

With over 20 years of experience in strategic planning, administration, management, and operations for corporations, foundations, and charitable organizations, Salvador develops strategic business infrastructure with holistic enterprise plans to facilitate workshops for client executive teams in compliance, leads, and orchestrates process refinement of operations, grant, and proposal writing, fund development, financial education, and more.

Salvador delivers a fresh approach to culture refurbishment in any organization through enlightened function and cohesiveness in individual and group dynamics. Her proven, customized, forward-thinking personal leadership coaching and team-building activities have garnered awards and acknowledgement from domestic and international organizations.

A distinguished leader with excellent diplomacy skills, Salvador has raised millions of dollars for various individuals, domestic, and international organizations; her work attracts results.

www.sharonsalvador.com

CHAPTER 20

FINDING YOUR FOUNTAIN OF YOUTH

Michael D. Butler

The idea of the Fountain of Youth has its origins in creation, when mankind was exiled from the Garden of Eden, and runs deep in the hearts of humans everywhere throughout the generations forward and backwards for thousands of years.

The Spanish explorer Ponce de Leon tried to find it, and plastic surgeons sell it *en masse* in a bottle, capsule, retreat, or surgery. Most everyone wants to look and feel great, so it's a huge market and always will be.

Born with Desire

The desire to live, grow, and prosper are placed within all of us before birth. The desire to walk, build, grow, and learn that grows into the desire to connect, love, create children, and leave a legacy never stops developing until we die. The desire to travel, explore, and discover new things currently has the human race pursuing the colonization of Mars and the Moon. Humans desire change over time, but the constant desire is the need for growth and expansion. The DNA of success is the divine thumbprint of an almighty Creator, and as humans, each of us possess it.

At age eighteen, I was ready to leave the house and start my life. Putting my name on the lease in college meant I could be the landlord and collect rent from my two college roommates. It also meant I was responsible for the rent if they did not pay. I desired freedom and discovered it was found in responsibility. Many in modern psychology will argue that desire cannot be changed; I disagree. I look at my own life and see how I fine-tuned and even changed my desires by changing my vision.

Desire Can Be Good or Bad

Desire is not evil or good. It is a God-given characteristic we are all born with. Some choose to use desire for evil, while others choose to use it for good. Desire—like hunger, the need for sleep, the drive for sex, and the drive to succeed—is neither good nor evil. Desire is normal and natural. The ethics and motives of desire can be judged in how humans choose to use their desire. For example, a parent can desire one path for their child, but true bliss will come for the parent and the child once the parent recognizes the uniqueness in their child and allows the child to make choices for themselves as they age - Experiencing the positive and the negative results of their choices.

How to Change Your Desire

How do we change someone's desire? We change their picture. Growing up in communist Poland, eight-year-old Ania's family had to wait in line weekly for toilet paper, flour, and salt. Fast forward a decade-and-a-half later, living on the beach in Naples, Florida, she would see how another side of life could be—the life of the affluent and the wealthy. She would quickly attain her goals by putting herself through college and going on to get her Master's and Doctoral degrees, opening a wellness spa, and opening a women's high-end fashion boutique that would bring former presidents of the U.S., other nations, and the famed fashion designer Oscar de la Renta into her store.

The Wright Brothers

Kittyhawk, North Carolina is the place the Wright brothers took their idea—flying a plane, and tested it to find eleven seconds of success. They did, indeed, go airborne, but only for eleven seconds. Many would call that a failure. They, however, saw it as a resounding success. Their vision for flight fuels our world economy to this day. I step on dozens of airplanes around the globe in a single month. The Wright Brothers defied the law of gravity with a greater law: the law of lift.

Desire Begins with Vision

My desire to run my first marathon was reborn in me at age thirty-nine-and-a-half. I had written it down as a bucket list goal when I was thirty and almost forgot about it. But when I ran across that notebook of bucket list items, the desire in me was reborn. I could feel, hear, and see myself crossing the finish line with my arms in the air and the crowd cheering.

Running My First Marathon

That very day, I laced up my shoes and ran one block and was out of breath. The next morning, I ran a block and two mailboxes, and I was gasping for air. I immediately knew what I needed to do.

That very second, I went home and googled "new running shoes," but I didn't stop there. I found and joined a running group in my city where three times a week and every Saturday morning at five or six a.m., we'd meet and do our long runs.

Laser Focus Mixed with Burning Desire

Running coaches will tell you that the optimal journey from "couch potato" to marathoner should take at least a year, depending on your age. I only gave myself six months to train, because my fortieth birthday was approaching, and it was my desire on my bucket list to complete my marathon before the age of forty.

Working with a Team of Mentors

I considered my running group of twenty young athletes—yes, I was the oldest in my group—to be my team of mentors. Most of them had run at least one marathon, and our coach had run more than 100. Even though I spent most of my time trying to catch up with "the pack," they pulled me—kicking and screaming at times—to new heights in my health, which would translate into business and in life.

There's no way I could have endured the long training runs of eighteen and twenty miles without them. The pain, the passion, and the fun conversations propelled me and motivated me to get out of bed at five a.m. on Saturday mornings in the twenty degree weather, because I knew they would hold me accountable. More importantly, I was holding myself accountable. The idea of the sheer boredom or running without them and the feeling of loneliness one experiences running alone fueled me to press myself to run 26.2 miles. I never could have done it without them.

Not only did I finish my first marathon, The Route 66 Marathon in Tulsa, Oklahoma before my fortieth birthday, but my four sons—Michael, Matthew, Joshua, and Jeremiah—all ran the last three miles with me, crossing the finish line with me, making that—apart from the days my sons were born—my greatest life moment ever.

What Do You Desire?

What is it you desire? What is it you want in life? What is it you really want? Go ahead and think about it for a moment. Close your eyes and visualize it. Ask yourself, *What do I really want?* Now, begin to see yourself achieving it. Write it down, speak about it, talk about it. Visualize it. Dream about it. Write it down and post it to your mirror and your refrigerator and inside your car and on your phone as your screen saver. Jim Rohn said, "We become what we think about most of the time." King Solomon said in Proverbs, "As a man/woman thinks in their heart, so are they."

I love the story of Caleb, the eighty-year-old patriarch in the Bible who told Moses, "Give me this mountain" that was promised to him at age forty. Many would have given up if they had not realized their dream in forty years, but not Caleb. Regardless of his age, he was still ready and willing to receive all that had been promised to him and his children. No matter what your age or station in life, now is the time to start, and don't give up until you have it!

Visualize what you want and take the necessary steps to achieve your dream, regardless of your setbacks or failure. Keep looking at the picture you have created, and keep moving forward.

In 1950, no one had ever run a four-minute mile. In fact, experts globally conceded that it would never happen, and the human body was not capable of running a mile in less than four minutes. But in the 1952 Olympics, in Helsinki, Finland, a twenty-three-year-old Brit named Bannister ran a 3:59.4 mile and forever changed the world's mindset about that topic.

He would only hold this coveted title for forty-six days, because, over the next year, more than 100 men ran a sub-four-minute mile, all because the glass ceiling of belief was shattered, and they believed they could. Once belief ignites, desire is born!

 **Michael D. Butler** has been a guest on Fox News, and USA Today and has gotten his clients onto CNN, Dr. Phil, TMZ, TLC, Rolling Stone, Entrepreneur Magazine, Inc500, TBN, TruTV, Fox Business, CBS, Forbes, NBC, Good Morning America, TedX Stages, Bravo TV, MD TV, and many others.

His Podcast, The Publisher Podcast is heard by thousands globally and features guests from Hollywood and the Literary Industry.

He has published 4 of his own International best-selling books in multiple languages: *The Single Dad's Survival Guide, Best-Seller Status – Becoming a Best-Selling Author in the Digital Age, The Speaker's Edge – Turning Your Part-Time Passion into Your Full-Time Speaking Career* and *It's Complicated – When Finding Love was a Matter of Letting Go.*

He Founded and runs 1040Impact.org that rescues kids in human trafficking, educates them and teaches them trade skills to equip them for life in Asia in places like Pakistan.

He is the CEO of Beyond Publishing with authors in 20 countries and over 400 titles by end of 2021.

www.MichaelDButler.com